Modular
Programming
and
Management

Modular Programming and Management

W. G. R. STEVENS

PALL MALL PRESS · LONDON
IN ASSOCIATION WITH
URWICK DIEBOLD LIMITED
COMPUTER CONSULTANTS

Published by the Pall Mall Press Ltd
5 Cromwell Place, London SW7

© 1969, U R W I C K D I E B O L D L I M I T E D

First published 1969

S B N 269 67191 9

Printed in Great Britain by
The Garden City Press Limited
Letchworth, Hertfordshire

Contents

1. Why Modules?

1.1 INTRODUCTION

This book has a twofold purpose. Firstly, it attempts to put programming in its correct place in the job of developing business computer systems, to state a set of objectives for the programming function and to indicate what is needed if these objectives are to be met. The greater part of this first chapter is concerned with these matters, and it is addressed mainly to executives, like chief accountants and data processing managers, who are ultimately responsible for the development of computer systems. No detailed knowledge of programming is assumed; attention is focused on the organisational and managerial problems.

However, the book has a second purpose. Chapters 2 to 7 describe in detail a method for organising the programming office and for producing programs; they form, in effect, a programming methods manual. This part of the book is addressed to those directly responsible for running the programming office, and assumes first-hand knowledge of programming in some high-level language like COBOL or PL/I.

For convenience, this method is called modular programming. No particular originality can be claimed for it as a method; it is a formalisation of what all expert programmers tend to do in practice anyway. In fact, the reaction of many programmers when they first hear it described is to say that they have been writing their own programs in modular form for years.

This misses the point. The object of this formalised version of modular programming is, firstly, to make it possible to deskill a large part of programming work; to relieve the present desperate shortage of experienced programmers by using people with less experience.

Secondly, modular programming, as described here, is harnessed to a method for getting management control of the programming function. Some managers seem to believe that programming is almost a religion and that the programmers, the high priests of the cult, cannot be subjected to the requirements of any earthly calendar. Programmers can, perhaps, be forgiven

1

for wishing to preserve this view of them and their work; but it is pure obscurantism, nevertheless. There is ample evidence that, with the right attitudes and the right tools, programming can be planned and controlled in much the same way as any other production process or office procedure.

1.2 THE PROBLEM

The chief obstacle to the satisfactory use of computers in business is the systems development problem; that is, system design, programming and implementation. Not only does systems development require a great deal of time and the services of expensive staff, but also it tends to drift out of control. Schedules are not met and actual costs exceed the budget; if, indeed, a budget is prepared in the first place.

Even when the system is running operationally, the troubles are not over. Systems frequently turn out to be disappointing in practice. Sometimes there is some unforeseen technical problem; very often, for example, checking and correcting the input turns out to be a larger problem than was anticipated. Sometimes management discover, when they start using the completed system, that it does not meet their needs; there may be enormous expenditure on solving the wrong problem. Another rude shock for management may come when they discover that the computer system has tied them into a strait jacket. Their freedom to change methods of working, as the needs of the business change, is severely curtailed, and may disappear altogether.

In short, it is commonplace to find that management are dissatisfied with their computer departments and it is not surprising that what evidence there is, in this notoriously difficult field, suggests that fewer than half the computers installed actually pay their way. Management may pay the bill for the computer and its minions, expecting an effortless ride on a magic carpet. In the event, they sometimes discover that they have bought a Juggernaut that crushes all before it and moves slowly and inexorably in the wrong direction.

There is no simple solution to these problems. In part, they are due to the shortcomings of computer staff and the methods they use; in part to inappropriate attitudes and actions on the part of management. To a much larger extent than is generally recognised, they are due to the inherent limitations of the very primitive computers that we are now using.

In consequence, before considering the programming problem, it is first necessary to set it in context; to look at systems development as a whole.

1.3 SYSTEMS DEVELOPMENT

When setting a computer to do a particular job, there are three separate and distinct tasks to be performed. Firstly, there is the need to decide exactly

2

what it is that the computer is to do; secondly, there is the job of programming the computer to do it; finally, there is the job of getting the whole system working on an operational basis.

For example, in a sales accounting application the first task would involve, among other things, deciding exactly how discounts are calculated, when reminder letters are to be sent to customers who fail to pay, and how soon after the end of the month statements are to be dispatched. The second task, on the other hand, would be concerned with whether the sales ledger is to be stored on tape or on disc; with the number of programs to be written and the function of each; and with writing and testing the programs themselves. The third task would entail training staff to prepare the system's input, to understand and use its output, and to operate the necessary controls.

Although the third task, generally called implementation, is very important, we are only considering here the first two tasks and the people who perform them; system designers and programmers.

In practice, it is still unusual, in a computer installation, to see any clear dividing line between the two tasks. While it is clear that the system designer (systems analyst) is more concerned with the first task and the programmer more concerned with the second, there is a great deal of variation between computer users. In one extremely well-known company which has pioneered many computer applications, the systems analysts usually produce nothing more than a brief outline of requirements, leaving much detailed fact-finding to the programmers. In another equally well-known company, the systems designers not only decide how many programs are to be written and how they are to be linked, they also produce a flowchart for each program which the programmers then take as their starting point. Other companies fail to recognise any difference between systems design and programming; the work is done by the project teams who are responsible for both.

In general, however, there seems to be no clear policy and one looks in vain for any clear statement of where the system designer ends and the programmer begins his work. For example, the Ministry of Technology booklet on staff titles glosses over the problem, as indeed do most computer users. What happens depends on the individuals involved and the time available.

It is obvious that a clear dividing line must be drawn between the system designer and the programmer. If this is not done, it is impossible to judge how well the system designer has performed, or whether he has even completed his task. In some installations the system designer always seems to finish his work on time, while the programmer is always late. This is a sure sign that, for the system designer, the work is completed when time runs out, and that the programmer is completing whatever the former did not have time to do.

If this dividing line is necessary, where should it be drawn? In fact, there are enormous advantages in making the system designer concerned exclusively with *what the computer is to do* and the programmer concerned exclusively in *making the computer do it*. There are several reasons for this.

Systems design—deciding
exactly what the computer
is to do

Programming—getting the
computer to do it

Implementation—getting
the system working in
practice

Fig. 1. Computer Systems Development

First, it makes it possible for the management of the department that is to use a computer system to participate in designing it. All too often, the system designers are computer specialists who produce the specification of a system in isolation and then carry out what is, more or less, a sales exercise in 'securing management acceptance'. In practice, management often accept systems without any clear idea of what they are accepting; they do not understand them in detail.

This understanding is crucial. It is virtually impossible for the system designer to gain sufficient knowledge of the facts to be sure that the system he is proposing is adequate in every detail; and details are often crucial. Elegant systems are often murdered by ugly anomalies; the need, for example, to produce a special report once a year. It is here that the manager's deep, first-hand experience is vital.

How is the manager to learn what the proposed system is to do? Even when computer technicalities have been eliminated, business systems remain hideously complicated. Before it is possible to perform any job on a computer, all discretionary elements must be reduced to rules and all the rules must be explicitly stated. If the job is not to be performed on the computer it is normally not necessary or even useful to be explicit; so the complexity of the system never comes to the surface. Where it is necessary to state all the rules explicitly, alarming documents like the Army Pay Manual are produced.

In consequence, it is almost impossible to gain more than a superficial understanding of any business computer system without having designed it or used it for some time. This is the primary reason why management must participate in designing a computer system. It is not feasible to wait until it

4

has been programmed and used for six months before management decide whether it is what they want; the only alternative is for management to participate in designing the system in the first place.

Even if the system designer does produce an adequate system, it is still useless unless those who use it are fully committed to it. Unless they participate in designing the system, it is possible that the moment an operational difficulty is encountered the response will be to reject the system wholesale. Of course, this is very unusual. Users in general will give a system a more or less fair trial; but it is bad policy, all the same, to let them occupy the judge's chair. The system should be the users' system as much as it is the system designers'.

One reason why management participation is the exception and not the rule is that system designers tend to be technical experts, who talk in their own incomprehensible computer jargon. *What* the computer is to do becomes tangled with the details of *how* the computer is to do it; but it is only the former that is any primary interest to management. A manager, however, has to grapple with both if he is to participate in the design of a system. It is difficult enough for him to understand a complex system specification; matters are made worse if it is written in the jargon of a technology with which he has, at best, only a nodding acquaintance. It is not surprising that so many well-intentioned managers end by throwing up the sponge and accepting the system designer's specification on trust, or mistrust, as the case may be.

One attempt to escape from this difficulty, often seen in practice, is to give the managers some elementary training in programming; an alarmingly large amount of so-called management training in the computer field consists of this and nothing more. Elementary programming is, in itself, quite an interesting subject, and it is very easy to teach; it is perhaps of some value in demonstrating the powers and limitations of the computer. However, teaching managers to write programs is a partial and unsatisfactory solution to the communication problem; the only real answer is to hand the technical problems over to the programmer, leaving the manager and system designer free to concentrate on the vital details of what the system is to do.

The second reason, closely related to the first, for separating system design and programming in this way, is that different skills are required. The programmer must be an expert at converting requirements into efficient computer programs. He must be an expert at communicating with machines; his ability at communicating with people is of secondary importance.

The system designer, on the other hand, needs skills over and above this. Certainly, he needs the programmer's analytical ability, if not the programmer's technical knowledge; but, for the system designer, human skills are paramount. He must be able to overcome any initial suspicion, to elicit

5

information from people who are probably not expert communicators; to distinguish fact from opinion. Besides, system design always seems to involve the exploration of some dark corners; even in the best-run businesses there is always the odd skeleton in the cupboard, some hidden piece of muddle or inefficiency. To make matters worse, the system designer is generally not responsible to the management of the department he is operating in; often he is seen as an irresponsible meddler, unaware of the real problems of daily operating. Perhaps, too, the system designer sometimes casts himself in the role of avenging angel whose job it is to expose inefficiency and muddle and to see that the unrighteous get their just deserts.

What this means is that the system designer must possess a rare combination of analytical ability and tact; it is ridiculously wasteful to have such people spending time on irrelevant technical considerations.

The third reason for defining system design and programming in this way is that the one must precede the other. A great deal of time and effort can be wasted at the programming stage by what are politely known as 'system changes'. As often as not, these are not changes at all; the programmer in the course of his work simply discovers a gap in the system specification which must be plugged before he can proceed. This not only causes much effort to be wasted, worse than this, it jeopardises the efficiency of the system, as, inevitably, the overall design has been based on an incomplete knowledge of what the system is to do.

Closely associated with this is the fact that constructing a schedule for system design is far more difficult than constructing a schedule for programming. Once a clear and complete system specification has been written, the task of programming it can be planned and scheduled with reasonable accuracy. Completing the design of the system before programming begins means that those parts of the job to which the greatest uncertainty attaches are done as early as possible in the schedule.

If this division between system design and programming is accepted, the end result of the system design operation must be a system specification which is a complete and precise statement of what information is to go into the system, what is to come out and what the connection between them is to be.

Unfortunately, there is at present no completely satisfactory method of specifying systems. Most methods currently in use both underspecify in the sense they are not precise enough, and overspecify, in the sense that they get involved in programming strategy.

System specifications tend in practice to suffer from one of two vices. On the one hand, some specifications are much too vague and wordy; they are little more than an outline of requirements. On the other hand, when greater precision is attempted, the result tends to be unintelligible, and more like a computer program.

The reasons for this are, firstly, that system designers are often ex-programmers who find it hard to leave programming behind. Secondly, the most commonly used tool for specifying systems is the flowchart, which originated as a method for documenting programs.

The decision table has sometimes been regarded as the solution to these problems. True, it represents an advance, but only a small one; the over-all problem of binding together a set of flowcharts, decision tables and input/ output definitions to form a coherent whole has not been finally solved.

Various attempts have been made to improve matters; the ADS method developed by NCR is a good example of how traditional methods may be improved. A more radical approach has been adopted by Mr C. B. B. Grindley and the author in *Systematics*. However, it must be admitted that a completely satisfactory method does not yet exist, and much development work needs to be done.

Objectives

To make productive use of the programming
and computer capacity at his disposal
To meet target dates
To produce reliable programs
To produce programs that can be modified

Symptoms of failure

Missed target dates
Delayed or inaccurate results due to
program error
Delays in modifying programs
Excessive computer usage for program
testing

Fig. 2. Objectives for the Programming Office Manager

1.4 OBJECTIVES IN PROGRAMMING

If, then, we have defined programming and separated it from system design what objectives can be set for it? How can we tell whether the programming office manager is doing a satisfactory job? There are four main objectives that can be identified for him.

Firstly, he must make the most effective possible use of the resources at his disposal. The only two resources he has that are worth considering are the programmers themselves and the computer capacity required for program development.

The programmers will probably vary greatly in skill and experience. At the moment, it is a most difficult personnel problem to establish and maintain a team of experienced programmers. Not only is there a constant demand in advertisements in the press for experienced programmers, but also it seems that every programmer wants to become a systems analyst. Furthermore, considering the rate at which new computers are being installed, it seems very likely that the situation will get considerably worse before it gets any better.

The programmers vary in skill and experience; similarly some parts of the work to be done require a great deal of skill and experience, other parts require very little. For example, designing a suite of programs is difficult; coding a well-planned routine is easy. This point is discussed in detail later, but suffice it to say for the moment that with conventional methods the programming office manager has an insoluble problem. He is bound to make very skilled people spend a great deal of time on very easy tasks. Similarly, he will, on occasions at least, be forced to give an inexperienced programmer work that is too difficult for him. One of the greatest advantages of the modular programming method is that it brings the right skills to bear at the right time.

The other programming resource, time for program testing, is very often a bone of contention between the programming office manager and the operations manager. Time spent in program testing is unproductive; this does not matter very much if the computer has a substantial amount of spare capacity as the marginal cost of computer time is very low. However, once the computer is fully loaded, time becomes scarce and it is clearly the programming office manager's job to see that the most effective possible use is made of the time consumed.

Secondly, the programming office manager should ensure that the work of the programming office is properly planned and controlled. He should be in a position to schedule a job accurately in advance, and to control progress against the plan. He should be able to see that a schedule is not going to be met while there is still time to take corrective action.

In practice, it is unusual to come across a programming office with anything approaching an adequate planning and control system. What is even more unfortunate is that failure to meet target dates is frequently taken philosophically as something that cannot be avoided. As was said earlier, programming is felt to be a special activity, which cannot be made subject to any normal method of process control. This is, of course, nonsense.

Thirdly, programs should be produced so that they are reliable in use. It is inevitable that some program errors should arise in the course of operational running which were not detected previously during program testing. However, these can be kept to a very small number if testing procedures and controls are adequate.

Fourthly and finally, the programming office manager should ensure that programs are capable of being modified when the need arises. This is a very important, but neglected, subject. All businesses respond to changes in their environment and consequently their information processing systems must be able to change, too.

To summarise, the programming office manager is subject to much the same considerations as any other office manager in the business. There is no reason to let him hide behind a technical smokescreen and pretend that the performance of his programmers cannot be controlled or that a satisfactory product cannot be produced. In general, he has got away with it up to the present, but only because computers were new and unknown. He should not be allowed to get away with it any longer.

1.5 MANAGEMENT IN PROGRAMMING

It is obvious that a good systems specification is essential if a satisfactory performance is to be achieved in the programming area. It is not possible to produce a program, or anything else, efficiently and on time, while what is to be produced remains in question. This is true whether modular programming is adopted or not; it is the first of the two principles on which any good programming system must be based.

The second essential principle to successful programming is the provision of adequate management.

Generally, a programming project is carried out by a team of subordinate programmers working under a senior programmer who is responsible to the programming office manager. As will be seen, this is the case with modular programming as well. Both the programming office manager and the senior programmers are, beyond question, managers; at least, if the classic definition is to stand: 'a manager is an individual who is accountable for more work than he can do himself and who gets some of it done through other people'.

Therefore, planning the job, motivating the programming team and controlling the work against the plan must be the programming office manager's primary task. Unfortunately, he is too often selected on his technical programming ability, and his training is confined to technical matters. The author knows, in fact, of only one training course in the whole of the country which sets out to teach a programming office manager how to run his team.

In view of this, it is not surprising that so many programming office managers, let alone the senior programmers, regard themselves merely as master craftsmen; people who are better at writing programs than their subordinates. It is not to be wondered at that the management of many projects is so lamentable; if nobody regards management as part of his job.

9

In practical terms, the programming office manager must be selected almost entirely on his managerial ability; senior programmers must also have supervisory skills. If there is substantial doubt in any particular case, it is imperative to employ the programmer concerned in some other capacity, such as software programming. On the other hand, it should be borne in mind that management, at the senior programmer level at least, is a pretty elementary business. Its techniques can very quickly and easily be taught, and, in general, only a programmer suffering from a positive personality defect could fail to learn them.

1.6 CONVENTIONAL METHODS

In most programming offices there is a document called a standards manual. It contains instructions to the programmer on such matters as how to organise his flowcharts, what the different shapes he can draw with his template are to be used for, what notes are to be included in the text of his program and so on.

A great many of these standards manuals are almost entirely useless. There are several reasons for this.

Firstly, the manuals are often too vague; they contain instructions like, 'flowcharts should go into sufficient detail to indicate what the program is doing', and tend to drift off into giving unctuous good advice without telling the programmer what to *do*.

A manual should instead contain instructions like 'each box on the flowchart may represent a number of source statements, but including, at most, one sequence change statement'. In this case there is very little room for argument about whether a programmer is carrying out instructions or not,

Secondly, many manuals describe documentation procedures only. It is. of course, essential that programs are adequately documented, but documentation standards help only with maintenance—they do not help in achieving the other objectives in programming.

Thirdly, unless documentation standards are linked to a system for scheduling and controlling the job, documentation will be neglected. Every programming office with an inadequate control system suffers from panics as a matter of routine. Program documentation is the first casualty in these cases as 'we can always do the documentation later'. In practice, of course, the next panic comes along too soon and the documentation never gets done.

For all these reasons a great many standards manuals gather dust at the bottom of somebody's drawer, and, indeed, even if they were followed rigorously they would make only a partial contribution to solving the problem.

1.7 MODULAR PROGRAMMING

Everything that has been said so far applies to all programming offices. Adequate system specifications and senior programmers with supervisory skills are always necessary. Without them, modular programming will be as unsuccessful as any conventional programming method. What, then, is the basis of modular programming and what advantages does it offer?

Modular programming is based on an analysis of what is difficult about programming. Most newcomers to programming start their training with a course lasting for a few weeks and provided by a computer manufacturer. On this course they learn a little about flowcharts, but the bulk of the course is taken up with learning to code instructions in a particular programming language. There is nearly always some practical work included; the trainees write and test at least one short program.

The reaction of the able trainee to a course like this is often surprise. Why, he asks, is programming supposed to be so difficult? Has he not already learnt how to write and test programs? What more is there to learn?

Of course, disillusion is at hand. The trainee returns to his employers and is given a program of, say, 500 instructions to write, which is perhaps ten times as large as any programs he wrote during training. At once, he finds his flowcharts sprawling uncontrollably from sheet to sheet, program switches multiply alarmingly and soon he is floundering in his program like a fly in a spider's web.

The point is that it is not at all difficult to write and test a program of fifty high-level statements—say, two coding sheets—in a day. Any moderately competent programmer can do it. On the other hand, to write a large program at the same rate, fifty fully tested statements per day, is a fantastic achievement. In practice, even the very best programmers in the most favourable circumstances rarely work at more than twenty-five statements per programming day.

The fact of the matter is that writing a program of 500 instructions does not merely take longer than writing a program of fifty instructions; it is very much more difficult. Program construction, that is, dividing a program into a set of logical routines with clear and simple connections between them, is the hardest thing that a programmer has to learn.

It takes a long time for some programmers to grasp this fact. They will say, for example, that program testing is the most difficult part of programming. This is not so; difficulties in testing almost disappear if a disciplined approach is adopted, and in any case many of the residual difficulties are due to poor construction in the first place.

Programmers like to think of their job as an art. If anything justifies this

11

MODULAR PROGRAMMING SUMMARISED

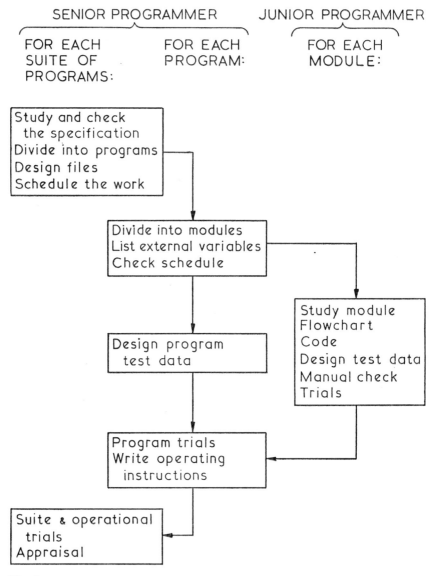

Fig. 3

12

view, it is the difficulties of program construction, for this is the area in which experience and judgement count for most and formal training least.

In modular programming, the senior programmer, when given a system specification to implement, first divides it into programs and designs the necessary files to link them. This is, of course, normal practice. However, instead of distributing the programs to be written among his subordinates and probably retaining one or more to write himself, he further divides each program into sub-programs or *modules*. It is these modules that he distributes among his subordinates for separating and writing and testing. Later he stitches the completed modules together to form a suite of programs. Figure 3 expresses this schematically.

In this way, the senior programmer himself does the most difficult parts of each program, handing the simpler tasks down to the junior programmers. Putting it another way, he converts a few big difficult programs into a lot of small easy programs.

Simple as this technique is in outline, it creates a number of very formidable technical problems, as it is necessary for the senior programmer to specify the modules to be written very precisely. The bulk of this book is concerned with describing a method for overcoming these difficulties. In addition, it describes a method for planning and controlling the work of a programming office; giving the senior programmer some of the tools that he needs to do his job.

Before going on to discuss the method in detail, it is worth considering the disadvantages and advantages of using the modular programming method.

1.8 DISADVANTAGES

Modular programming cannot be adopted without an upheaval in the programming office. It is likely that some of the more experienced programmers will dislike the idea of not coding the programs they plan. Similarly, if a programmer who has been used to writing complete programs is told to start writing modules instead, he is likely to be disgruntled.

These problems resolve themselves in time. As trainee programmers, without experience of writing complete programs, are taken on, they find writing modules a natural and interesting occupation. As the senior programmers learn to use the modular method, so they see its advantages working in practice.

However, the difficulties in getting modular programming adopted in the first place must not be underestimated. It is fatal to attempt to avoid these difficulties by a compromise; to say, for example, that all modules in a particular program will be written by the same junior programmer. True, this

13

will immediately make the senior programmer's job easier, as he no longer has to define the modules so precisely. But what in fact happens is that the junior programmer's job is made correspondingly more difficult, and this defeats the purpose of the method.

Without a good deal of discipline, at least in the early stages, an office using modular programming will tend to drift back into using conventional methods. If this happens, then the whole exercise is pointless; it would have been better not to start.

Of course, for the most part, the necessary discipline can only be exercised by the senior programmers. It is therefore very important to make sure that they are fully committed to making the method work.

The first disadvantage of modular programming, then, is the initial difficulty in getting it adopted. The other disadvantage is the training problem. One of the objectives of modular programming is to give inexperienced programmers work that is within their capabilities, while preventing them from doing work that is too difficult for them. How, then, will they ever learn to do the more difficult job, without actually doing it? Where do tomorrow's senior programmers come from?

This problem can be solved by planning. A potential senior programmer can work with an experienced senior programmer on a project or two and then run a project of his own under fairly close supervision. This, of course, takes time; it should not be left until there is a desperate shortage of senior programmers.

In fact, this disadvantage can even be construed as an advantage. Firstly, when using modular programming, it is not necessary to give an untried programmer the difficult task of constructing a complete program. Until he has worked in the office for six months or a year, and the programming office manager has had time to assess him, the amount of damage he can do is strictly limited. Secondly, one of the reasons why programmers take so long in learning to construct programs adequately is that they take a good deal of time to see the problem. Modular programming does not, and cannot, provide a foolproof formula for good program construction, but it does identify the problem.

1.9 ADVANTAGES

The advantages of modular programming will emerge as the book proceeds. This section attempts to summarise them. Of course, any planned approach to programming will produce many advantages, principally:

1. The programs are produced on time; or, at least, if the schedule slips, there is an advance warning that it will do so.

2. The programs are adequately tested before operational use, and so only rarely fail when running.

What advantages does modular programming offer, over and above these? There are three that can usefully be identified:

1. Programmers work in smaller units; a programmer is given a module to write, about two days' work, not a complete program, which may take up to six months. Not only does this make control easier, but it also gives flexibility in deploying and re-deploying resources. In emergencies, programs can be produced at enormous speed, simply by piling in more programmers to write the modules. For example, in one case, a program containing more than 1,500 high-level language statements was written, tested and made operational in ten working days.

In addition, management are not so vulnerable to staff changes. With normal methods, it is practically impossible for one programmer to take over another's half-completed program. With modular programming, a programmer produces a complete and usable module every few days; the work wasted, even if he leaves without notice, is minimal.

2. The active life of programs is extended. Each program consists of a number of clearly separated modules. Modification can be carried out quickly and easily; the time that passes before programs need rewriting can be extended; when rewriting finally becomes necessary, there is a good chance that some modules can be salvaged from the wreck and used again.

3. More effective use is made of the scarcest resource. There is no shortage of good trainee programmers. They can be selected, pushed through a basic course and set to work in less than twelve weeks. What is so desperately lacking is programmers of eighteen months' or two years' experience. This is due partly to the fact that there were fewer computer installations two years ago, and partly to the fact that good programmers tend to move to system design. What modular programming enables us to do is to make thrifty use of their skill and experience. It has been amply proved in practice that, using modular programming, two experienced programmers and four beginners can produce work that matches, in quantity and quality, the work of five experienced programmers.

1.10 CONCLUSION

Ever since it was first seen that programming was a problem, various solutions have been peddled. Once, it was claimed that the programming problem would disappear as soon as computers were available with sufficient immediate access memory to contain a complete program. Then people pinned their hopes on high-level languages; some still do. Another great hope was software of various kinds; to trace the course of a program; to produce a symbol index; to generate a flowchart from the program text. Just at the moment, the idea of using on-line terminals for program development is beginning to capture people's imagination.

All these devices are of some service and often can be used profitably, but the fact remains that people, in general, look in the wrong direction for solutions. The programming problem is managerial. It consists in getting a group of people with different levels of skill and experience to co-operate in getting an intractable (and fundamentally unsuitable) machine to do a complex and often ill-defined task, while keeping to a schedule.

There is no technical device to solve this problem; it is difficult to see how there ever could be one. It is fascinating to see that what interests many people about modular programming is the technical problem of providing harness for independent module testing. This is even considered the chief problem in getting modular programming to work: 'If only we had suitable harness, we could do modular programming and all our troubles would be over'.

In fact, the modular programming method described in this book is an attempt to solve the managerial problems associated with programming; and managerial problems require managerial solutions.

2. Planning the Suite

2.1 CHECKING THE SPECIFICATION

The first task of the senior programmer responsible for implementation of the system specification is to check it.

He studies the specification in detail to see if it appears to be complete and precise. Naturally, he cannot be completely sure that the specification is correct, for that would involve carrying out his own system investigation. However, he can draw the system designer's attention to places where the specification is unintelligible or self-contradictory, or where his own knowledge of the business indicates an error or omission.

In this connection, system test data is important. It should be provided, both the input and the expected output, by the system designer. Ultimately, it is used for checking that the programs do what the designer intended, but it is also valuable to the senior programmer at this early stage, as it gives him a method of checking that his understanding of the system specification is correct.

The senior programmer takes the specification on the one hand, and the test data with expected output on the other. He then works through them both, checking that they are consistent with each other.

At the same time, the senior programmer judges whether the junior programmers working on the project will be able to understand the specification. It must be borne in mind that they probably have less business experience than the senior programmer, and will need more detailed explanations.

The result of these checks will almost certainly be that the senior programmer refers a number of points back to the system designer. It is extremely important that such queries are resolved and the specification amended at once.

There are, generally speaking, very strong external pressures at this stage to start programming. These pressures must be resisted until a satisfactory system specification has been produced. If programming is allowed to begin before this, then it is overwhelmingly likely that the work done will have to be either scrapped or re-hashed when the system is properly specified. If the former, it is work wasted; if the latter, the programs become confused from the outset.

In consequence, although it is always pleasant to announce that programming has begun, it is a pleasure that must be deferred until the job that the programs are to do has been adequately defined.

2.2 THE OVERALL STRATEGY

It is now necessary to divide the total job into a number of programs linked by files. This is the most important single task in the entire programming operation, as mistakes made at this stage are very difficult and expensive to rectify later. The following considerations should be taken into account.

Computer memory size. Obviously, each program or part of a program must be sufficiently small to fit into the memory of the computer that is to be used. It is useful to estimate the memory that each program will require under the following headings:

(*a*) Software
(*b*) Input and output areas
(*c*) Major data items—arrays, etc.
(*d*) Program, minor data items, etc.

If this method is followed, the task of estimating program size is not so difficult as it might seem. The internal memory needed for (*a*), (*b*) and (*c*) can be calculated with complete precision, and between them, these may well account for half the total memory required. This leaves only (*d*), the memory for the program itself, to calculate. Skill and experience are needed to calculate program size accurately but it is reasonable to expect the total of (*a*), (*b*), (*c*) and (*d*) to be sufficiently accurate to avoid gross errors when dividing the suite into programs.

Processing speed. The planned suite of programs should operate at an acceptable speed. An estimate is needed of the running time of each program, in relation to some convenient unit of input or output. What this unit should be will vary with circumstances, but it should be related to the system, rather than to the program. In an order processing application, for example, the running time of the input checking program could be estimated in relation to an order, where an order is input on a batch of cards. This would be better than estimating the running time per card.

Ease of operating. Computers work in micro-seconds; computer operators work in minutes. One reason why so many third-generation computers did not, in practice, work much faster than the second-generation computers they replaced is that operator time remains the same. It takes just as long to load stationery into a 1,500 line a minute printer as it did into a 300 line a minute printer. For this reason, when planning a suite of programs, a watch should be kept on operator time required. It is worth setting up a list of standards for a particular installation, for example, an overhead of ten minutes might be allowed for each program, and of five minutes for each magnetic tape to be loaded.

Insurance against error. Consideration must be given to what happens if a program fails through operator, computer or program error. The senior programmer must assure himself that in these cases the job can be restarted with a minimum of re-running time. This is particularly important when a long report is being printed, as a single missing page, due to a forms wreck, may make it necessary to reprint the entire report, unless suitable restart procedures have been devised.

Some thought, too, should be given to file security procedures, transcribing disks or preserving generations of the tapes. Though important, this, however, does not usually affect the programming strategy.

These four considerations in some cases conflict with each other, and then the senior programmer has to prepare a satisfactory compromise. The senior programmer records his solution by preparing the following set of documents.

Suite plan—see Fig. 4. Columns of the diagram are assigned to the various files, magnetic tape, magnetic disk, etc., that the program will read and write. In most cases, it is fairly clear when a collection of data constitutes a file; for example, a disk unit very often contains several files. However, in some cases, the senior programmer has to decide arbitrarily whether a collection of data constitutes one file or more. Different generations of the same tape file should be given separate columns.

On the left-hand side of the diagram each row is assigned to a program. The program's primary input, punched cards, etc., and its printed output are listed.

It is now possible to indicate which programs use which files by writing in the body of the diagram.

R indicates that the file is read by the program
W indicates that it is written
B indicates that it is both written and read.

It is therefore possible, by looking horizontally across the sheet, to see

SUITE : JOB PLANNING

PROGRAM No	PROGRAM NAME	PRIMARY INPUT	PRIMARY OUTPUT	T1 Vetted input (unsorted)	T2 Vetted input (sorted)	T3 Component Master file	T4 New Component Master file (updated)	T5 Output file (unsorted)	T6 Output file (sorted)
J01	INPUT & DATA VET	JOB CARDS	ERROR REPORT(1)	W					
J02	SORT 1	/	/	R	W				
J03	MASTER FILE UPDATE	/	ERROR REPORT(2)		R	W	W		
J04	SORT 2	/	/			R	R	W	
J05	OUTPUT LISTING	/	JOB LISTING					R	

Fig. 4

which files a program uses; or by looking vertically down the sheet to see which programs use a particular file.

File definition. The layout of all records of all files is now specified, together with notes on the sequence and organisation of records within the file. With high-level programming languages, record layout is best specified by using the language itself; in other cases special stationery must be used.

The expected and maximum possible size of each file is specified in terms of the media to be used. For example the expected size of a file stored on tape might half a standard length tape; the expected size of a file stored on disk might be twenty-five cylinders.

Program notes. A very brief description and the estimated memory requirements of each program are recorded.

Timing notes. The estimated running time of each suite of programs is recorded. This includes both computer and operator time, and all assumptions about file and input volumes are stated.

These documents, then, record the solution to the first programming problem, dividing the job to be done into a number of programs.

2.3. SCHEDULING THE JOB

At this point the senior programmer produces a schedule for the job, which shows what resources have been assigned to it and how long the job is expected to take.

The whole subject of scheduling and control is dealt with in Chapter 7.

2.4. AGREEING THE PLAN

The overall plan and the schedule for implementing it are now discussed in detail with the departments that are to use the proposed system and with the computer operating function. The system designer has a vital liaison function here.

Of course, the system itself must already have been agreed with the user departments before the senior programmer started his work. The purpose of the present discussions is to make a final check, especially on the questions like the cycle of operations and its timing.

The operating function has to be convinced that the proposed system can be worked satisfactorily, and that it will fit into the computer's work schedule.

It is important that work does not proceed until all concerned—the user department, the system designer, the senior programmer and the operating department—are convinced that the proposed suite of programs will do the job satisfactorily. It is also important that contact is established between the user department and the computer operating function. Eventually, they will have to co-operate to make the system work; so the sooner they get together, the better. They should not meet for the first time on the day the system becomes operational.

The documents on which the decision to go ahead is made, that is, those described in Section 2.2 and also the schedule for programming it, should be kept, unmodified, for reference. This ensures that there will be a clear statement of what was planned, against which to measure what is, in the event, achieved.

2.5 IMPLEMENTATION PLANNING

A vital, but often neglected, task is planning the way in which the computer will take over from whatever system preceded it. This must include a wide range of activities; for example, file set-up or conversion, staff recruitment, staff training and customer education.

These problems are outside the scope of this book. However, it should be noted that once a program suite, and the schedule for programming it, have been agreed, then its implementation can be planned in detail by the system designer and the user departments.

3. Planning the Program

3.1 What is a Module?

The program is now divided into modules. Every executable statement in the program belongs to exactly one module; that is every statement belongs to a module and no statement belongs to more than one module. By 'executable' is meant a statement that manipulates data or controls the flow of the program, for example 'add', 'read', 'print', 'call sub-routine'.

The other statements in the program, those that define files and records within files, and those that reserve memory for particular data items are considered later.

All the statements in a module are eventually coded so that they fall together in unbroken sequence in the program. The program, in effect, consists of blocks of instruction and each block is a module.

The main restriction on the structure of a module is that it may have one entry point only. Within a module, of course, control may be passed from statement to statement quite freely by means of sequence change statements, like 'go to' and 'if . . . then . . .'. However, when control is passed to another module, it must always be passed to the first statement of that module. This rule goes a long way to formalising the relationships between the modules. This point is illustrated in the left-hand part of Figure 5.

3.2 Internal and External Variables

In modular programming two kinds of data item are distinguished. Firstly, there are those that are used by one module only; these are called 'internal data items' or, more accurately, 'internal variables'. Secondly, there are those that are used by more than one module; these are called 'external data items' or 'external variables'. Figure 6 illustrates this.

Putting it another way, modules communicate with one another by means of external variables; internal variables are merely for storage and calculations within the module. The tendency is for the external variables to be the

23

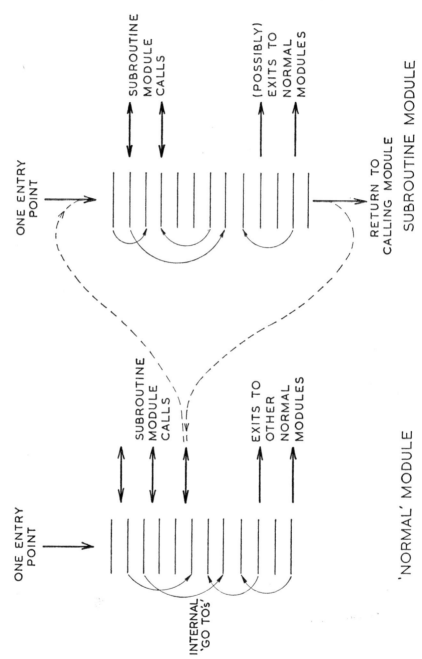

Fig. 5

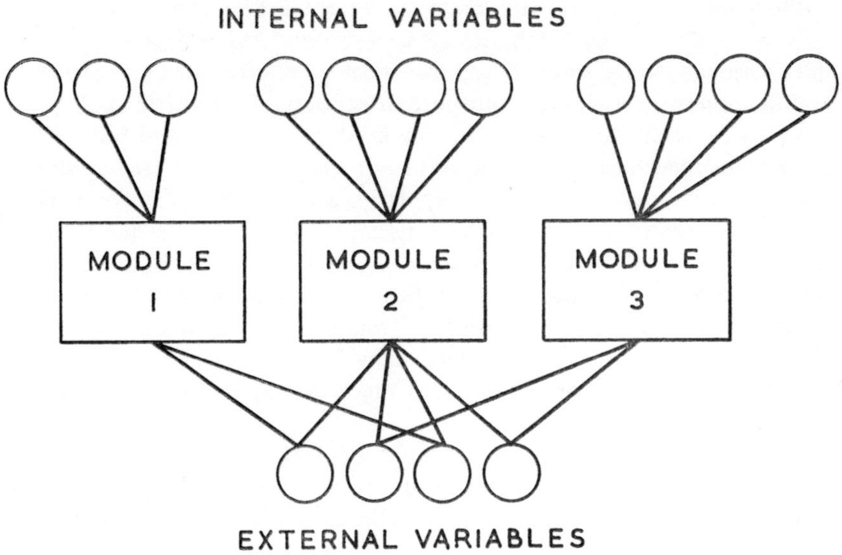

INTERNAL VARIABLES

EXTERNAL VARIABLES

Fig. 6

ones that are logically the most important, and for the internal variables to be more concerned with the tactics of programming.

An external variable is a variable used by more than one module. It is helpful to distinguish between the different ways in which a particular module can use a particular variable. These are:

Reference. The module does no more than refer to the variable; the module may test it or add it into a counter, but does not modify it in any way. For example, this will be the way in which a tax calculation module will use a tax code. A tax code is never changed by a tax calculation module; it is merely used.

Modification. In this case, the module simply modifies the variable; the previous value of the variable has no effect on the outcome. For example, a module may set a variable equal to zero or to some other variable. Here the variable's previous value is lost and does not affect the new value.

Both. In many cases a module both refers to and modifies a particular variable, sometimes in different statements but often in the same statement. For example, a module that adds 1 to a counter both refers to and modifies the counter; the counter's value changes, but its previous value contributes to the new value.

25

It follows, of course, from this that every external variable must be modified by some module or other, otherwise it is never modified and so is not a variable. Similarly, every external variable must be referred to by at least one module, otherwise it serves no purpose; it is not used for anything.

It may be useful to draw an analogy between programs and modules. A program handles files of information; some are input, some are output and some are both input and output. Similarly, a module may handle a file or files; but in addition it will handle external variables by referring to them, modifying them, or both. In a sense, then, external variables are part of a module's input and output. This can be shown by supposing that, for some reason, a program were split into two programs, with some modules going to one and some to the other. Then, many of the external variables would have to become input or output; it is the only way in which the modules could communicate.

Finally, there is one small exception to the rules given above: all data items that are used for input or output purposes (printed output apart) count as external variables. For example, suppose 'hours worked' are being read from punch cards. The data item 'hours worked' into which the hours are read is for convenience treated as external, even if it is not passed on to any other module, but merely added into a total.

3.3 SUBROUTINES AND PARAMETERS

One of the qualities of a good programmer is that he uses subroutines freely to help him construct his programs. By contrast, the bad programmer uses programmed switches instead; in fact it might almost be possible to measure how well constructed a program is merely by calculating the ratio of subroutines to programmed switches.

For this reason, there are in modular programming two kinds of module:

The normal module which is entered by means of an ordinary sequence change—'go to'—statement.

The subroutine module which is entered by means of some kind of 'call' or 'perform' statement, or even, perhaps, by a function reference.

If a module (of either kind) calls a subroutine module, it should be noted that this does not violate the 'one entry point' rule given previously. The rule that a module may only be entered at the beginning does not apply to re-entry after executing a subroutine. Figure 5 illustrates the two different kinds of module.

The use of parameters creates another minor problem in the use of subroutines. It is generally possible in high-level programming languages to have two kinds of variable within a subroutine. Firstly, a subroutine may refer directly to a data item just like any other part of the program. On the other hand it may refer to dummy variables—parameters—which are equated with different data items on the different occasions on which the subroutine is executed. For example, a subroutine may perform a calculation on three dummy variables, X, Y and Z. If the statement calling this subroutine is, say:

CALL SUB (A, B, C);

then the subroutine will in fact operate on A, B and C; if, elsewhere in the program, there is a statement:

CALL SUB (L, M, N);

then the subroutine will operate on L, M and N instead.

In modular programming, the rule is that modules communicate with each other only by using external variables. This could be interpreted to mean that all variables mentioned in a 'call' statement as well as the parameters themselves must be external. In fact, it is better to interpret it as meaning that only the parameters need be external. In the example given, this would mean that X, Y, and Z were classed as external variables, but A, B, C, L, M and N could be external or internal variables, or even constants or arithmetic expressions, if the language used permitted it.

There is one further point to make. Parameters and subroutines are a very useful device for sealing part of a program into a water-tight compartment. Since this is the object of modular programming, it would be very desirable to make parameters the only means by which modules communicated with each other. Certainly, it would make it easier to move a module from one program to another. Unfortunately, however, it seems that, for the moment, this is not possible; the resulting programs are not efficient enough. We, therefore, have to adopt the compromise system recommended here.

> Size 25–75 statements
> Simple linkages
> Few external variables
> No coding duplication
> Useful in other programs
> Suits programmer's ability
> Change isolated
> 'Logical' part of program

Fig. 7. Criteria for Modules

3.4 CRITERIA FOR MODULES

Obviously any program may be divided into modules in an enormous number of different ways. What advice can a senior programmer be given on how to do it? There are no hard and fast rules about how a program should be divided, but there are a number of considerations which he should take into account:

Size. A module should not comprise more than seventy-five or fewer than twenty-five source language statements.

Linkages. The pattern of linkages between modules, both the 'go to' type and the subroutine calls, should be as simple as possible.

External variables. The program should contain as few external variables as possible.

Coding duplication. The duplication of coding in the different parts of the program should be avoided; for example, by using subroutine modules.

Generality. Those parts of a program that are required for use, or seem likely to be required for use, in other programs should be isolated in separate modules.

Programmers' ability. A module should match the ability of the programmer who is to write it; it should be neither too trivial nor too complex a piece of work for him. The problems of designing trial data and testing the modules requires particular attention.

Isolate change. Those parts of the program that seem likely to be changed in the future should be isolated in separate modules.

Of course, these criteria conflict; it is always possible to reduce the number of external variables and to simplify the linkages merely by having fewer, larger modules. Similarly, by making the modules small enough it is always possible to make them usable in other programs and to avoid coding duplication. The senior programmer has, in fact, to secure a diplomatic compromise between a large number of conflicting requirements. Even when he has done this, there will still be room for differences of opinion about whether he has found the best compromise. In fact, it is probably worth mentioning one more consideration:

Logic. Each module must be 'logical' part of the complete program.

This is a very vague requirement, but what it amounts to is that the way a program is broken into modules should correspond to the way in which a senior programmer would describe the program to somebody else. The modules should be organised in a way that makes sense.

It should be made clear that this job of dividing a program into modules is not a new and difficult job that did not exist before modular programming. A program always has to be divided into sections of some kind; it may be done well or badly, formally or informally, but it is always done. And furthermore it is a vital job. If it is done badly and the resulting program is a tangled mess, rather like a plate of boiled spaghetti, then the program is almost certain to be unreliable in use and impossible to modify.

The problem of good program construction, therefore, is always with us. What modular programming does is to drag it into the open and put it in the hands of somebody competent to deal with it.

3.5 DOCUMENTING THE MODULES

Once the senior programmer has divided the program into modules he records what he has done on a set of standard documents. These are:

Program plan. This is fundamentally a flowchart with one box assigned to each module. Subroutine modules also have boxes assigned to them but no attempt is made on this document to show how they are used. Figure 8 contains an example. Note that a pre-printed flowchart is used, instead of drawing all the boxes and lines with a template. Boxes are linked either with a vertical arrow (e.g., M01 and M02) or with a pair of horizontal arrows and a bus bar (e.g., M02 and M06).

There are two reasons for preferring this kind of flowchart to the conventional kind. Firstly, standard templates will not draw boxes large enough to contain more than a few words; this is true of the rectangular boxes, and the situation is even worse in the case of the other, totally unnecessary, fancy shapes. Secondly, it takes a good deal of time to draw a conventional flowchart. When the flowchart needs to be redrawn, as every flowchart does at least once during the course of program development and several times afterwards, the tendency is to skimp the work; to cramp the new boxes into an odd corner, or, more commonly, to omit them altogether. The pre-printed flowchart, on the other hand, has adequate writing space in each box, and, when it needs modifying, it can be redrawn in a few minutes.

In short, there is no doubt that the conventional kind of flowchart can be

29

PROGRAM / ~~MODULE~~ FLOWCHART   REF *J01*

~~from~~

Open output file. Read first card. End job if it is not a batch card.	M01

Not O.K. — Check batch leader card. If O.K. read first detail card in the batch	M02

↓ Batch card O.K.

Check detail card. Report all errors found.	M03

Batch Card / Detail Card — If no errors in detail card, condense it & write it on the tape output file. Read next card.	M04

↓ No more cards

Print batch analysis. Close output file and end the job.	M05

Batch Card / No more cards — Report error on batch card. Read cards looking for the next batch card.	M06

Subroutine for checking that a field contains either blanks only or numeric digits only - no alpha.	M07

NOTES OVERLEAF: YES / NO

Fig. 8

EXTERNAL VARIABLE GRID SUITE: JOB PLANNING PROGRAM: J02							
VARIABLE	DIMS	M01	M02	M03	M04		
VK DATE		M			R		
FA NAME			M	R	R		
FA HOURS			M	R			
FA TYPE			M	R			
FA DATE			M	R			
FC NAME				M	R		
VA TOTAL				B	R		
VS FINISH			B		R		
VK WEEK	10			B	R		

Fig. 9

31

superior, if there is leisure to draw it and if what it represents will never change; in real life, however, the pre-printed form has marked advantages.

Returning to the example, it will be noticed that a brief description of each module is written in the box assigned to it. What is written requires careful thought and should consist of fifteen to twenty words. In addition a code is assigned to each module, M01, M02, M03, etc. Modules that are to be used in other programs do not follow this system but are given a coding comprising M and two letters, e.g., MAB, MBC, etc.

External Variable Grid. The purpose of this document is to list all the program's external variables and to indicate how the different modules use them. It is analogous to the Suite Plan described in Chapter 2. Figure 9 contains an example. The modules are listed across the top and the names of the external variables down the side. Both subroutine and normal modules are listed, but not the subroutines' parameters. For assigning names to the variables, a system is used which is a compromise between normal mnemonic systems and coded systems. The first two letters of the name follow a convention; the rest form a mnemonic. For the first two letters, the convention is that all variables that form part of input or output records begin with F. The second letter denotes which file the variable belongs to. Thus, all variables in input or output records are prefixed FA, FB, FC. . . . All other external variables begin with V. The second letter is K, if the variable is used to store values; A, if it is used for arithmetic; and S, if it is a switch.

This system overcomes the main objection to using pure mnemonics, which is that, in a program of any size, it is often desirable to give the same name to several different variables. In practise, this gives rise to confusing and arbitrary variations. For example, Customer No. might be in one file CUSTNO; in another CUSTOMER; in a third CUSTNUM; and sometimes despairing forms like KUSTOMER will crop up.

Under the system described above, however, a customer number might be read from a master file into FACUST and from a transaction file into FBCUST. It might be stored for sequence checking purposes in VKCUST, and loaded into FCCUST for output, on, say, a printer. The names are different; but the differences are meaningful, not arbitrary.

If the variable is an array, its dimensions are specified in the space provided.

When the external variables have been entered down the side of the grid, the codes of the modules are entered across the top. The relationship between modules and external variables can now be stated by writing R, M or B in the appropriate square. R, M and B stand for Reference, Modify or Both as described in Section 3.2.

A useful way to proceed is to fill the grid in column by column, that is considering one module at a time; and to check it row by row, that is one

SUBROUTINE GRID

SUITE: *JOB PLANNING*
PROGRAM: *JO3*

CALLING MODULE	W06	W07	W08
M01	X		O
M03	X	X	O
M05			X
M06			X

Fig. 10

33

MODULE DESCRIPTION

PROGRAM : J03   MODULE : M08

PARAMETER	R/M/B	DESCRIPTION
VK CODE	R	CUSTOMER CODE WITH MODULUS II CHECK DIGIT

EXIT TO:	CONDITION
CALLING MODULE M03	NO ERROR DISCOVERED ERROR IN CUSTOMER CODE

SPECIFICATION: SEE P.30 OF SPEC FOR CODE CHECKING PROCEDURE.
SET VSCODE TO I IF ERROR; TO 0 IF NO ERROR

Fig. 11

external variable at a time. A check can be made, firstly to see that each external variable is used in more than one module and secondly that it is used at least once and modified at least once.

Subroutine grid. The purpose of this document is to establish which module calls which. On the left is listed any module that calls any subroutine module. This list can, of course, include subroutine modules, as one subroutine can call another. Across the top are listed all subroutine modules. Figure 10 contains an example.

Relationships are now established by entering X and O in some of the squares:

X indicates that the module to the left calls the module above directly.

O indicates that the module to the left calls the module above indirectly e.g., it calls some third module which in turn calls the module above. In Figure 10, M01 calls M06 and M06 calls M08. Therefore, M01 calls M08 indirectly.

The effect of this is that by looking along a row we can answer the question, 'If this module moves to another program, which subroutines must it take with it?'

Module description. For each module a document is prepared giving a list of parameters (subroutine modules only) and a specification. Figure 11 contains an example.

Ideally this specification consists of a set of references to the system specification eked out with brief notes. In some cases, however, more detailed notes are required; and in extreme cases, where perhaps an inexperienced programmer has to be given a difficult module, a flowchart of the module may be needed.

It is important to keep control of this operation. If references to the system specification prove inadequate for more than twenty per cent of the modules designed, then probably something is wrong. Either the senior programmer is dividing programs into modules on the wrong basis, or else the system specification is sub-standard.

3.6 AMENDING THE SCHEDULE

When the senior programmer has divided all the programs in a suite into modules, he is able to re-estimate the amount of programming work involved.

The method for carrying out this procedure is described in detail in Chapter 7.

4. Writing the Modules

The previous two chapters described how the suite is divided first into programs and then into modules. They also described the preparation of the various documents that the junior programmer uses. These are:
For the suite:

Suite plan

For each program that he is concerned with:

File layouts
Program plan
External variable grid
Subroutine grid

For each module that he writes:

Module description
Description of any module called by the module he is writing

Obviously, many of these documents will be needed by several different programmers. The suite plan does not, in most cases, need duplication; it can be pinned to the office wall. All the program and module documentation, however, must be duplicated, preferably by photocopying.

The originals of all the documents produced should remain with the senior programmer. The junior programmers should use duplicates only.

It is vitally important that these documents are altered, should alteration be necessary, by nobody except the senior programmer in charge of the project. He is also responsible for seeing how each junior programmer has a completely up-to-date set of documents.

Junior programmers are, of course, free to make suggestions and comments; in fact they must be encouraged to do so, but they must not be allowed to deviate from the documentation they are given, unless the senior

36

programmer first alters it himself. If this discipline is not maintained, then modules will be produced which are incompatible with each other. Modular programming then becomes impossible.

The junior programmers, as far as possible, work on one module at a time, writing and testing it before starting the next. It may be, though, that delays at the testing stage will make it necessary to start work on another module before the first is completed. A certain amount of overlap of this kind is unavoidable and does no harm.

4.2 FLOWCHARTING

When given a module to write, the junior programmer's first task is to draw flowcharts of it. The principle adopted is that, instead of one large piece of paper, the programmer uses several small pieces which form a hierarchy. No flowchart may have more than ten boxes on it. An example of one of these flowcharts is in Figure 12. It is the same pre-printed flowchart that was used for the program plan.

The boxes on the flowchart are of three kinds:

1. Plain box. This indicates that the operations performed are not shown in any more detail on another flowchart.

2. Box with double line right-hand end. This indicates that the operations described in the box are shown in more detail on another flowchart.

3. Box with subroutine module code at right-hand end. This indicates that a subroutine is called at this point.

The basic rule is that a flowchart documents a group of statements with only one entrance and that via the first statement. In a sense, therefore, each flowchart describes a sub-module.

In practice, then, there is always one flowchart giving an overall picture of the module. In the case of very small modules, this might be the only flowchart, and all boxes would be of type 1 or 3.

However, with most modules, this top-level flowchart will also contain some type 2 boxes, and for each type 2 box there will be a second-level flowchart. Some of the boxes on these second-level flowcharts may possibly be shown in greater detail on third-level flowcharts. It is unlikely, however, that a fourth level will ever be reached. In Figure 12, for example, the whole module is represented by five boxes. The third box is to be expanded and shown in more detail on another flowchart. The fourth box is a subroutine module call. The remaining boxes are plain; no further details of the operations to be performed are given in flowchart form.

It should be noted that it is not permitted to skip a level. If a particular box needs expanding into, say, thirty boxes, then it is not enough to produce three flowcharts each with, say, ten boxes on it. There must be an intervening

37

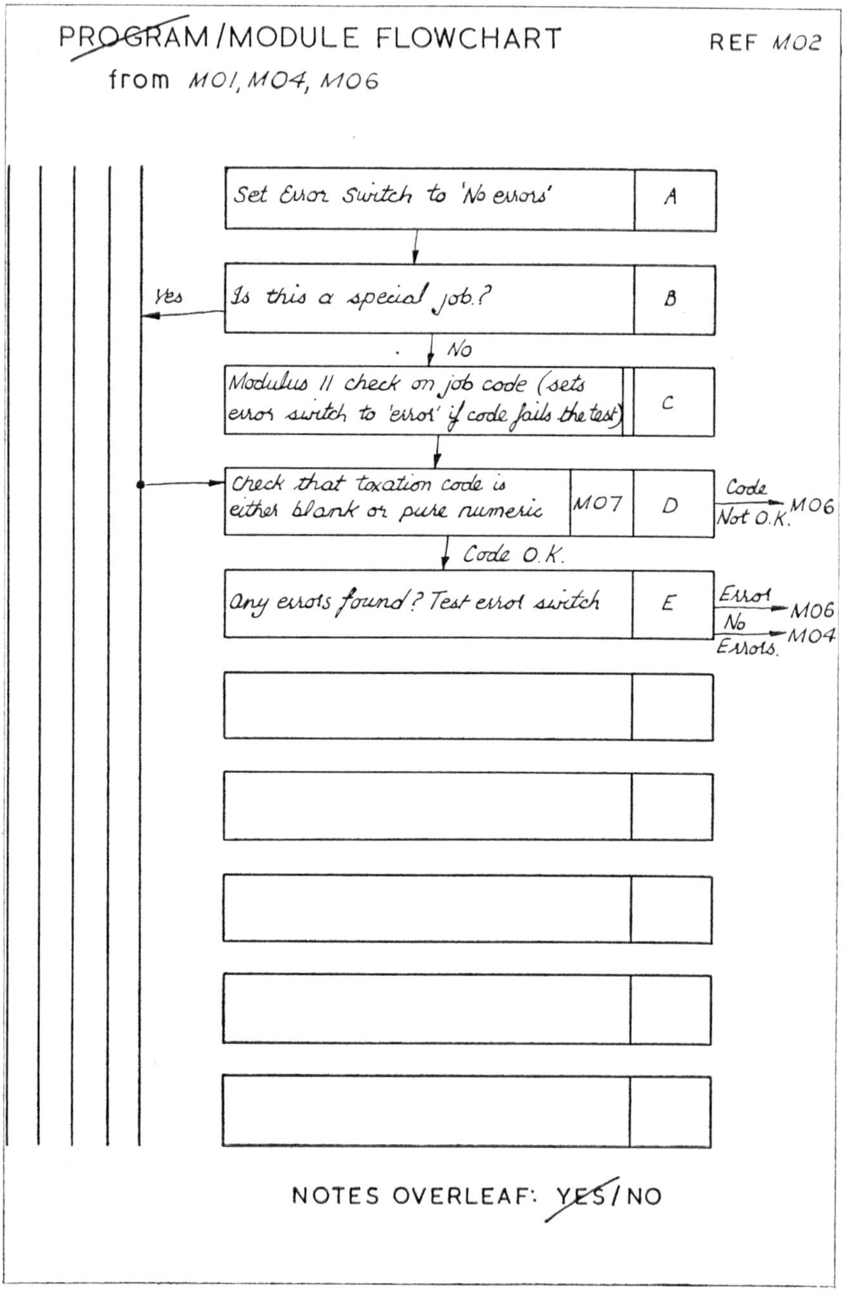
PROGRAM/MODULE FLOWCHART
REF M02
from M01, M04, M06
Set Error Switch to 'No errors'
A
Yes
Is this a special job?
B
No
Modulus 11 check on job code (sets error switch to 'error' if code fails the test)
C
Check that taxation code is either blank or pure numeric
M07
D
Code Not O.K.
M06
Code O.K.
Any errors found? Test error switch
E
Error
M06
No Errors.
M04
NOTES OVERLEAF: YES/NO

Fig. 12

flowchart containing three boxes, one for each of the three lowest level flowcharts.

This hierarchical structure is firmly linked to a reference system. In the top level the boxes are labelled A, B, C. . . . If, say, box B is shown in more detail on another flowchart, the boxes of this second-level flowchart will be labelled BA, BB, BC. . . . If, in turn, box BC is shown in more detail, labels BCA, BCB, BCC . . . are used.

If the flowchart is the top flowchart in the hierarchy and so represents a complete module, the module code is written in the top right-hand corner. If it is lower in the hierarchy, the module code is written as before and, in addition, the code of the box that is being expanded; B, BC, DE, etc.

The bus bars on the left are used as with the program plan to indicate transfers within the flowchart itself. Transfers out of the flowchart, either to different modules or to different flowcharts in the same module, are indicated by arrows leading to the right. Each arrow is tagged with the code of the module or flowchart concerned.

Similarly, all the different points from which the flowchart may be entered are listed at the top. In this way, each flowchart's relationship with all the others is made clear; we know how this flowchart can be reached, where it can lead to and where further details of the operations to be performed are found.

In this way, the policy of dividing the program into water-tight compartments is extended below module level. A module is divided in flowcharts in something of the same way that a program is divided in modules. The only difference is that there is no attempt to introduce hierarchies into the internal variables. Variables are not confined to flowcharts in the way in which some variables (i.e., the internal variables) are confined to modules.

There are two further points that sometimes cause difficulties when the more powerful high-level languages are being used.

The DO/FOR *statement.* Statements for setting up loops should be represented by one box each. The statements inside the loop can then be expanded, if necessary, on another flowchart. This second flowchart, if drawn—this point is considered later—need not, of course, show the DO/FOR statement or its related END statement, if there is one.

Compound IF *statements.* In some languages facilities exist for building into an IF statement a whole set of statements to be executed, if the condition is true. It may also be possible to build into the IF statement, a set of statements to be executed if the condition is false. In both cases, the IF statement should be shown in a single box with further expansion in another flowchart, if necessary. The condition need not be re-stated at the lower level. When both

39

the IF and the ELSE clauses need further expansion the original IF statement must be spread over two boxes and not one.

What must be avoided in both these cases is the common practice of translating these compound statements into simple statements for flowcharting purposes; for example, by drawing the flowchart as if a loop, actually controlled by a DO statement, were controlled by three separate statements; which set, increment and test a counter.

There is also the question of how detailed flowcharts ought to be. Without a firm rule on this point, programmers tend to produce flowcharts containing insufficient details. This is not a question of idleness; the fact is that something which seems blindingly obvious to a programmer when he first draws the flowcharts may not be at all obvious to somebody else in a year's time. Unfortunately, a programmer is rarely convinced of this until he has had the experience of trying to understand a program that he himself has written a year previously. And by then the damage is done.

The simplest and most easily enforceable rule is that flowcharts must come down to a one statement per box level. This is a good rule to apply initially when programmers are inexperienced, either in programming or in the modular method. A relaxation of this rule that may be worth introducing later is to say that a box, at the lowest level, can contain more than one statement, but not more than one sequence change statement. Sequence change statements include GO TO, IF . . . THEN . . ., CALL and DO.

Finally there is the question of what text should be written in the boxes. Much very painstaking flowcharting is of no use at all, simply because it repeats what is in the program text. For example, no trained programmer will learn anything from a flowchart that states:

'Add 1 to subscript VKMAN'
'Divide VATIME by 60'
'Set Switch 1 off'

when he can see in the program text:

VKMAN = VKMAN + 1;
VATIME (VKMAN) = VATIME (VKMAN)/60;
VSERROR = 0;

Obviously, we need a statement of what is being done; not how the computer is doing it. The three statements in the example are much better documented by:

'select next man'
'convert the time he has worked to hours'
'set error-on-card switch to "no errors" '

It is difficult to formulate rules for the text that is written except to say that no names of variables, VKMAN, VKTIME and VSERROR, in the above example, are to be used in flowcharts. As a general guide, though, what is written should indicate the purpose of the operation rather than its mechanics. For example: 'convert the time he has worked to hours', is better than 'divide the time he has worked by 60'. A point often overlooked is that, although flowcharts prepared by system designers are meant to be a complete explanation of the system, those prepared by programmers only serve to explain or document a program text. They are not intended to be used independently of the program text, or by people who do not understand the programming language.

4.3. CODING

If the flowcharting operation has been adequately carried out, then coding presents few problems. The planning of the module has been completed, and the programmer is left free to concentrate his attention on using the programming language accurately and without grammatical mistakes. Delaying the coding in this way is very beneficial, and contrasts strongly with much programming office practice.

The programmer has to assign labels to statements and internal variables (labels have already been assigned to external variables, of course):

Statement labels. The flowcharts have already provided a referencing system that can be taken over wholesale: A, B, BA, BCA, etc. Since, of course, the same label will crop up in a number of different modules, it is necessary, when no suitable software is available, to prefix the label with the module code in order to avoid ambiguity: M06A, M06BA, etc. However, this should be avoided if possible.

In many cases several labels can be used to refer to the same statement, for example: B, BA, BAA all refer to the first statement in box B of the top level flowchart. In this case, the shortest form B, should be used.

Internal variable labels. The same combination of code plus mnemonic that was used for external variables should be adopted. Instead of prefixes VK, VA, VS there should be used YK, YA, YS. As with statement labels, it may be necessary to use the module code instead of Y if the available software cannot cope with duplicate labels in different modules.

The rules for using coding sheets must depend on the language used, but in most cases these rules can be applied:

41

1. One statement, at most, is to be written on each line of the coding sheet.

2. Internal variables are to be defined in a group at the beginning of the module.

3. Statement labels are to be on the left in a column not used for anything else. It should be possible to pick them out merely by running the eye down the left of the page.

Current programming languages always provide the facility for inserting comments in the text of the program. This facility can be used, at the programmer's discretion, but it must not replace the flowcharts as a form of documentation. There are several reasons for this.

Firstly, if the comments are to provide adequate documentation by themselves they will increase the length of the program text, and hence the punching load, by a factor of 4 or 5.

Secondly, when a program is being modified during testing or later, comments tend to be omitted or scattered. They are an extra complication when the programmer is trying to produce a 'clean' modified program.

Thirdly, having a hierarchy of flowcharts at different levels is a great aid to understanding the program. Comments in the text of the program are necessarily all on the same level, and are correspondingly less useful.

Finally, detailed flowcharts are necessary, to all except the exceptional programmer, as an aid to developing good program construction. The view that flowcharting is an added burden, requiring time and effort over and above that needed to produce the program, is quite false. Since flowcharts are needed as a development tool, they can usefully be extended to serve as a documentation method.

In most cases, the programmer will have to code a short routine in which he embeds his module in order to test it. Generally speaking, it will read data and print results, in which case it can be coded before test data is designed. If the test data is to be presented to the module by means of, say, a DO statement with a list, then it will be necessary to delay parts of the coding until test data is designed.

Providing this test routine is often regarded as an overhead even to the extent of making modular programming impracticable unless special purpose testing 'harness' is available. With present-day software and high-level languages, this is not so. Perfectly satisfactory results can be obtained provided that care is taken.

On the other hand, of course, testing 'harness' is an advantage, and if modular programming is to be adopted it is worthwhile to obtain some, either from the manufacturer or from a software house or even by writing it.

4.4 MODULE TEST DATA

Module test data has one purpose only: to check that the module does what the junior programmer intends it to do. The test data and the routine in which the module is embedded for testing purposes, simulate the action of the rest of the program.

In fact, when designing the test data, most beginners provide, at the same time, too much and too little. They provide too much because the main paths through the module are tested and over again, and too little because some paths, for example, error conditions, are not tested at all.

The object, then, is to test all paths through the module and also the most common combinations of paths. Within these restrictions, the smallest possible quantity of test data should be prepared. It should be noted, though, that while the first requirement, to test all paths, is clear and explicit, second, to test the most likely combinations, is not. It is open to interpretation, and for this reason, the senior programmer should pay close attention to what his subordinates are doing in this area.

It should be noted, though, that when it is carefully planned, the actual volume of test data needed is often surprisingly small. This is because there is no need to make the module test data realistic; to get the proportions of ordinary and exceptional cases correct. There is no point in testing the same path through a module dozens of times.

As a check that there is adequate test data, the arrows joining boxes on the flowcharts should be marked. It is necessary to mark the arrows and not the boxes themselves as Figure 13 shows. There, three pieces of test data are needed to test every path, though at first sight it might appear that one is adequate.

Calculated results are essential, as without them the programmer will only be able to detect gross errors; errors that produce plausible results will escape him. For this reason, software for generating random test data, where it exists, should not be used.

The way in which test data and calculated results will be recorded must vary from module to module and must also depend, to some extent, on the programming language and software used.

The junior programmer hands his completed test data and the expected results to the senior programmer. This provides a valuable check, both that adequate test data has been prepared and that the junior programmer has understood the senior programmer's intentions for the module.

As soon as the senior programmer has indicated that the test data is adequate, the junior programmer can proceed to the testing operation, described in the next chapter.

43

TEST DATA

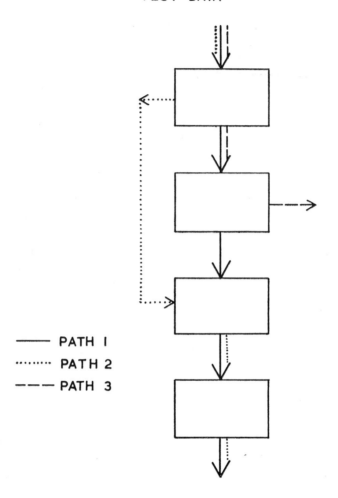

PATH 1
.... PATH 2
——— PATH 3

Fig. 13

4.5 GENERAL PURPOSE MODULES

The next two sections are concerned with modules that are not produced by writing them in the way previously described. These are general-purpose modules and modules produced by special-purpose module generators.

General-purpose modules, that is modules which can be used in more than one program, can be of many different kinds. However, they are exceptionally useful for file handling. There are various reasons for this. Firstly, it is commonplace to have different programs to handle the same file, secondly, it is often necessary to compress data in order to make the best use of the storage available. This means that the programming needed to handle the files has to be correspondingly complex and often needs to be in a low-level language. Finally, many program modifications affect files and the routines for handling them. It is an advantage to have one module only to modify; not two or three different modules.

File handling, then, gives scope for the use of general purpose modules. Other opportunities for using them exist, but there are no general rules. The situation varies from application to application.

How much programming work can be saved in this way? A great deal depends on the nature of the application and also of the size of the machine in use. In normal circumstances it would be unusual to reduce the programming workload by more than ten per cent.

The procedure for handling general-purpose modules is simple. The senior programmer in charge of a project, in the first place, should consider whether there are any previously written modules which he can use. Secondly, he should design his programs in such a way that duplication of coding between different programs is avoided. Finally, he should make some intelligent guesses about future programming work to be done, to ensure, that, if possible, modules written now will be of use later.

4.6 Special Purpose Modules

It should be obvious from what has gone before that there is no reason, if the available software permits, why different modules should not be written in different programming languages. Modular programming, as described here, was designed with high-level languages in mind, but it may sometimes be desirable, in the interests of efficiency, to write some modules in a low-level language. This, as we have seen, is most likely to be the case with modules that handle files, as many high-level languages are notoriously inefficient in this respect.

There is a further extension of this idea, which belongs to the future. It would be very desirable to have software for generating special purpose modules, much in the way that software is now available for generating, for example, sort programs. Two examples of this are file control modules and decision table modules.

File control modules. In essence, what Report Program Generators provide is a system for handling a file. The software reads a file, record by record and calls various subroutines, written by the user, in accordance with what is found. For example, the user might supply three subroutines for handling three different kinds of record; he will also supply subroutines to be executed

45

when particular control breaks occur; for example, if records are sorted by man within area, an end-of-man, an end-of-area, and an end-of-job subroutine would be supplied.

The great advantage of such generators is that they relieve the programmer of a good deal of time-consuming and error-prone coding. In the example given above a programmer writing this routine in any normal programming language would have to ensure that the end-of-man routine was executed not merely at the end of each man but also at the end of each area and at the end of each job. Programs very frequently fall into this pattern, and a good programmer soon learns to handle such situations. However, producing the necessary coding, always takes time and is always open to trivial error.

These Report Program Generator systems, which at the moment produce a program, could be greatly increased in power and flexibility, if the generator produced instead a control module to link together a number of other modules supplied by the user. No such system is at present available, but it might prove to have all the advantages of a Report Program Generator without any of its inflexibility.

Decision Table Modules. It would also be desirable to have software to generate decision tables as modules. In fact, when facilities for compiling decision tables are built into high-level programming languages, this facility may become available automatically. The external variables would be, of course, combined to form the conditions of the table; the actions would probably be exits to other modules, subroutine module calls, or perhaps statements in the programming language itself.

File control and decision table modules are just two examples of what could be achieved. The idea could well be extended to the field of applications software, where the modular approach, or something like it, is becoming quite common. The disadvantage of much applications software produced in the past is that the user has had to have all of it or none of it; were such software produced as a set of clearly defined, linked, modules its use could be increased enormously.

There is almost unlimited scope for modular programming in helping to reduce the fantastic amount of duplication of work which still goes on, despite the efforts of the software producers.

5. Testing

5.1 PRINCIPLES OF TESTING

It is very hard to explain to anybody without first-hand experience of programming, why it is that the programmer's carefully coded instructions should actually contain mistakes. It is easy enough to see that a trainee programmer might misunderstand a particular statement or facility in the programming language, but why do programmers go on making trivial mistakes in their programs, year after year?

The fact is that human beings are at a disadvantage when concentration and painstaking accuracy are required. Certainly, a year or so spent writing programs tends to alter, though not necessarily lower, one's opinion of human mental powers. It is while program testing that the revelation comes. The program, so carefully written, is submitted to the scrutiny, not of another person, but of a thorough, literal-minded and—mercifully—unemotional machine.

Certainly, among programmers themselves, program testing is regarded as a heroic struggle against the powers of darkness and chaos. Programmers are fond of telling tales, sagas sometimes, about how this or that suite of programs was tested; about the hours worked, the sleepless nights and the quantities of black coffee and benzedrine consumed.

In view of this, it seems churlish to suggest that the testing might have been more effective and completed sooner if it had been properly planned and if it had been preceded by methodical manual checking. The fact is, though, that program testing on the computer will inevitably be a wild and uncontrolled operation unless steps are taken to ensure that there are very few errors to remove in the first place. There are three principles of testing that must be adopted for a successful outcome.

Firstly, there must be a methodical approach to program or module writing, like the one described in the previous chapters. This not only reduces the number of errors in the program, it also gives the program a coherent structure, making it easier to locate residual errors. Secondly, the program must be thoroughly checked before it goes to the computer. Thirdly, there must be a systematic and leisurely analysis of each test run on the computer before proceeding to the next. These last two principles are discussed in this chapter.

The method described here undoubtedly takes some of the glamour out of program testing. But there are, after all, some advantages in making the job of getting a suite of programs to work less like Armageddon and more like hoeing a field of turnips.

5.2 MANUAL CHECKING

Manual checking should be performed using the program listing produced by the first compilation of the module. The advantages of using this instead of the hand-written coding sheets are that the programmer checks for errors made in punching the program and also that he is helped by the compiler's diagnostic messages.

The programmer's first job is to check for likely errors. This does not mean gazing at the program hoping that some error will reveal itself; to be useful it must entail working through a list of likely errors and checking that no statement in the program commits them. It is, for example, worth checking every statement in the program to make sure that when control is transferred, it is always transferred to the correct statement.

The list of standard checks should be developed by experience. It should be short, with a maximum of ten items.

The next stage is for two programmers, the author and another, to join forces to test the module. In effect, they play at being computers, driving the test data through the module. One, preferably the author, is responsible for keeping track of the values of the variables, while the other reads out the statements that form the module.

The best way of keeping track of the variables is to divide sheets of paper into columns and to assign a column to each variable. When the value of a variable changes, the new value is written in the variable's column. Thus, at any point in the checking process the value of a variable is shown by the last entry in the column. As the value of a variable changes, it should not be crossed or rubbed out; this makes the resulting document very useful later, when analysing the results of computer tests.

The main difficulty in adopting this technique is to get programmers to use it, but once it has been sold to them, the results are excellent; errors found during computer tests can easily be reduced to about one in every 150 statements.

It is worthwhile to keep a log of all errors that are discovered after coding has been completed. For each error there should be an indication of where it was found: checking for likely errors, test simulation, machine testing. A very brief description of the error should also be recorded. Of course, it must be clear to the programmers that this log will not be used to judge their performance, or errors will not get recorded. There are various advantages in keeping such a log. Firstly, when a programmer spends half a day in manual checking, he has something to show for it; it brings home to him the fact that a large amount of computer testing is avoided. Secondly, recording facts like this impresses them on the memory; programmers learn more quickly to avoid making the same mistake again. Thirdly, the log provides a means of setting up and maintaining the list of likely errors referred to earlier.

5.3 MODULE TESTING ON THE COMPUTER

It is worthwhile to compare the task of testing a conventional program on the computer with the task of testing a set of modules that will subsequently form a program to do the same job. The advantages of the modular method are:

1. The units to be tested are smaller, and, in consequence, locating errors is far simpler.

2. Most of the errors, typically three quarters, have already been removed by the desk checking.

3. The programmer has, as a byproduct of desk checking, a complete record of the changing values of each variable. This gives him a useful diagnostic tool.

4. If there are delays between test runs on the computer, the programmer is less likely to be left without anything to do. It is far easier for him to switch his attention to another module than to another program.

What this means in practice is that module testing is a relatively simple and quick operation. There are only two points to make about it:

Squeeze each test dry. A common fault is for the programmer to locate just one error in the program, correct it and rush on to the next test. On the contrary, the programmer should locate and correct all the errors that the test revealed.

Correct the flowcharts. This must be done before testing proceeds. One of the advantages of using the kind of flowchart described in Section 4.2 is that it can be discarded and re-drawn in a few minutes. With conventional flowcharts the temptation is not to amend them adequately, as it is such a time consuming operation.

If this approach, described here, is enforced it will be found that, even

49

if unlimited computer time is available, a programmer will be using only about four tests per day. Using more than this indicates, either that there are numbers of trivial errors which desk checking ought to have removed, or that the post-test analysis is being skimped. Progress control must involve analysing the log of computer trials to make sure that this kind of slap-dash testing is not taking place.

5.4 PROGRAM TESTING AND SUITE TESTING

When all modules belonging to a program have been assembled, the senior programmer fits them together to form a program. Most of the modules will have been specially written in the way described previously; some may come, with or without modification, from other programs.

Fitting the modules together, with most modern computers and software, is a fairly straightforward task. Where possible, linkage at an object language level should be adopted.

The senior programmer must have designed test data to test the complete program. It is not necessary for him to repeat the exhaustive testing that was carried out on the individual modules. His purpose is to check that the linkages are correctly made.

Following this, the senior programmer attempts to make the programs operate together as a suite, using the test data prepared by the system designer.

Any errors discovered during program or suite testing must be corrected by amending some of the modules. It is important that these errors be kept to a minimum; so analysing them is an important post-mortem operation.

The purpose, then, of this stage is to make reasonably sure that the suite of programs does what the system designer intends it to do. This is why system test data is so necessary and why the system designer should play a part in these tests.

The senior programmer's final task before proceeding to operational trials is to prepare operating instructions for the suite and its programs. Though very important, the form that operating instructions should take is outside the scope of this book.

5.5 OPERATIONAL TRIALS

Operational trials should be conducted, as far as possible, by people who will be responsible for running the programs operationally. The test data used should be, as far as possible, genuine data and not data invented for the purpose. As far as possible, it should be devised by user department staff.

The objects of operational trials are:

1. To check that the system meets the users' needs.

2. To familiarise user department staff with the new documents and procedures.

3. To familiarise the computer operators with the programs and to check that the operating instructions are satisfactory.

4. To discover how long it takes in practice to run the programs.

Where the computer system is replacing a clerical system, parallel running is desirable; that is to say, the two systems operate side by side and the results are compared. However, this is often not possible and some compromise solution has to be adopted.

5.6 APPRAISAL

There is little point in making plans of any kind, unless there is, later, a check on whether the plans work in practice. For this reason, there should be a job appraisal, preferably about two weeks after the suite has started running operationally. The purpose of this appraisal is to discover, by reference to the documents mentioned in Section 2.2, whether:

1. The time and resources needed to program the suite matched the original estimates.

2. The time it takes to run the suite operationally matches the original estimates.

In all but very large data processing departments, the data processing manager himself should carry out this appraisal. He uses for this, of course, information largely collected by other people, but he should satisfy himself that he understands the reasons for all discrepancies discovered.

A certain amount of diplomatic skill is needed here. On the one hand, a witch hunt atmosphere must be avoided; on the other, all computer staff must understand that they are judged on their ability to achieve specific objectives. Oriental fatalism—'schedules always slip 30 per cent', 'the first five operational runs always fail'—is out of place in a programming office. Of course, this appraisal of programming function is only part of the larger appraisal that a data processing manager must make of his entire department. The ultimate objective must be to establish an overall management by objectives scheme.

6. Maintenance

6.1 INTRODUCTION

System designers and programmers have a depressing tendency to lose interest in a computer system the moment it starts running on an operational basis. They see their job as development work; designing and programming system after system, always thinking about the future rather than the present.

This attitude is understandable but wrong. Every computer system is an investment made by the business. Throughout the system development phase it is a cost, pure and simple; no money can be made from it. The day the system starts running satisfactorily is the day on which, hopefully, it starts saving or making money for the business. It is odd, to say the least, that this is the day on which so many system designers and programmers should choose to abandon it. To put it more strongly: how can a system designer or programmer hope to improve his performance? He can only do so if he sees, at close quarters, the success or failure of his work, as it operates in practice.

In any case, almost every suite of programs that is run operationally more than a dozen times needs amending, at some time during its useful life. This job of maintaining systems on a useful, operational, basis should be regarded by system designers and programmers as at least as important as the job of developing new systems. All too often, however, it is pushed aside; it is done hastily and grudgingly and without proper planning or control.

Instead of sweeping it under the carpet, we should bring maintenance into the open. As a first step, it is useful to identify the four principal categories of amendments that are made to computer systems.

System Error. The programs do not do what the user or designer of the system intended. It may be that the system specification contained an ambiguity, though this ought not to happen if adequate system test data was provided. More probably, there was some error in the system specification due to a misunderstanding or oversight on the part of the system designer who wrote it.

A typical example of this kind of error might be that the system designer assumed that no customer would order more than twelve different products on any one day. A problem, large or small depending on circumstances, would arise if it were found in practice that some customers regularly ordered thirteen products and more.

Such errors come to light very soon after operational running begins. Correcting them is generally urgent; they tend to be the cause of major disasters.

Program error. A program does not do what the programmer intended. It is impossible to test a program with all possible pieces of input in all possible combinations; testing must, in practice, be performed by using a limited number of pieces of input in a limited number of combinations. Therefore. some program errors necessarily escape detection.

A typical error of this kind would be a program interrupting in mid-run because register overflows or a subscript runs amok. Alternatively, it might be that a cash amount is output as £1 27s 13d.

Correcting these errors is usually urgent. They may come to light at any time during operational running, but with decreasing frequency as time passes. Unfortunately, other amendments to the program breed errors of this kind; correct a major system error and there will probably be some program errors to correct within a few weeks. Therefore, although one might expect program errors to disappear completely, in practice they never do.

Improving Efficiency. Programs often need amendment to improve their operational efficiency, perhaps to enable them to handle larger volumes of input, or to take advantage of an expanded computer configuration.

These amendments are not usually urgent, unless inadequate planning allows them to become so.

Business Changes. All business organisations change as time passes; in consequence the computer systems that serve the business have to change as well. For example, a company might switch from a single price for each product to different prices for different customers. This would probably involve major changes to the invoicing program.

These business changes are, in fact, at the root of the amendment problem. If they did not occur, then computer programs would stabilise themselves and the need for further amendment would disappear.

As it is, however, programs tend to degenerate. The documentation gets out of step with the program text; the construction of the program gets weaker. Every successive amendment takes longer to implement and trails a longer string of other amendments in its wake. Soon, unless proper methods are used, there is nothing for it but to scrap the program and rewrite it.

Amendments brought about by business changes are sometimes urgent and sometimes not. Of course, bad programming or poor communications can make any amendment urgent. There is generally a deadline to be met; a new price structure might come into force on a particular date and the programs must be ready for it.

It is simply no good trying to ignore maintenance. Maintenance is a necessary and resource-consuming business; as a very rough guide, every 10,000 high-level language statements require the equivalent of one full-time programmer to maintain them. It is unusual to discover a programming office in which the average programmer spends less than one week in four on maintenance; it is often as high as one in two. Anybody who thinks that these figures are too high would be well advised to check the time recording methods used in his own programming office.

To summarise: the assumption that a program will require amendment must be built into the programming methods employed. Modular programming has many advantages; but simplifying amendment is one of the most important.

6.2 ORGANISING FOR MAINTENANCE

One of the main organisational problems in a programming office is that two different kinds of work have to be done. On the one hand, there is the job of developing new programs and making non-urgent amendments to existing ones. On the other hand, there is the job of making urgent amendments to programs the instant it is seen that they are necessary. This fire-fighting job, naturally, tends to disrupt schedules and jeopardise the success of development work.

One solution, frequently advocated, is to establish a special team of maintenance programmers, who are responsible for all amendments. There are considerable difficulties in this approach. Firstly, maintenance work requires greater skill and experience than development work. It can only be entrusted to good programmers; and good programmers, with few exceptions, prefer writing new programs to amending old ones. Secondly, the maintenance workload fluctuates; so the maintenance capacity is constantly too large or too small. If it is too large, a fill-in development job has to be found; if too small, development programmers have to take on maintenance work.

The result, in practice, is that you end with what you started with; a single programming team, only with a number of discontented programmers in it.

A more realistic approach is to spread maintenance work among all the programmers. As far as possible, maintenance should be planned in advance and built into the schedule like development. An allowance, which varies with circumstances, is made for fire-fighting maintenance. The whole question of planning work and allocating resources is considered in more detail in Chapter 7.

One of the advantages of using modular programming is that it is easier to fit both urgent and non-urgent modification work into the schedule. By making the junior programmer's unit of work a module, and not a program, it becomes far easier to schedule and re-schedule; to manipulate the available programming capacity to fit the work to be done.

A second advantage in using modular programming is that, just as it de-skills some of the development work, so it also de-skills some of the maintenance work. There is a senior programmer responsible for each program suite. As amendments become necessary, he decides which programs and modules need correction or rewriting, and he is able to assign the detailed work to the junior programmers, while retaining responsibility for the final result.

6.3 MAINTENANCE AUTHORISATION

All maintenance work should be planned by the responsible senior programmer working with, either the operations manager, or the system designer responsible for the suite. In general, the operations manager will request amendments to remove program errors, or to improve efficiency; the system designer will request amendments to meet changed user requirements, or to correct systems errors. Amendments, like all other programming work, should, of course, be authorised by the programming office manager.

It is an important point of principle that request for modifications should not go direct from the user departments to the programming office. Responsibility for the system requirements should rest jointly with the system design function and the user department; the programming office's responsibility is to embody these requirements in efficient computer programs. Therefore, the system designer must not be by-passed, as so often happens in some offices.

6.4 MAINTENANCE PLANNING AND CONTROL

Figure 14 shows a maintenance control form. It contains three sections. The first section contains the specification of the amendment and the second section the senior programmer's notes on how the work is to be done and how

55

```
┌─────────────────────────────────────────────────────────┐
│                                                           │
│              MAINTENANCE  CONTROL  FORM                   │
│                                                           │
│   SUITE: STOCK RECORDING   PROGRAM: P03                   │
│                                                           │
│   DATE OF  REQUEST: 2ND JUNE 1969                         │
│                                                           │
│   AMENDMENT  REQESTED BY:  BUYING DEPT                    │
│                                                           │
│                                                           │
│   DESCRIPTION: ALLOW FOR 20 WITHDRAWALS PER WEEK          │
│                INSTEAD OF THE EXISTING 5. SEE             │
│                          ATTACHED MEMO                    │
│                                                           │
│                                                           │
│   REQUIRED BY: 23RD JUNE 1969                             │
├─ ─ ─ ─ ─ ─ ─ ─ ─ ─ ─ ─ ─ ─ ─ ─ ─ ─ ─ ─ ─ ─ ─ ─ ─ ─ ─ ──┤
│                                                           │
│   METHOD: REWRITE M02, M03 (2 DAYS EACH) SEE             │
│           DESCRIPTION SHEETS LINK MODULES                 │
│           AND TEST (1 DAY)                                │
│                                                           │
│   STANDARD  TIME,  5   MAN/DAYS                           │
├─ ─ ─ ─ ─ ─ ─ ─ ─ ─ ─ ─ ─ ─ ─ ─ ─ ─ ─ ─ ─ ─ ─ ─ ─ ─ ─ ──┤
│                                                           │
│   ACTUAL TIME:  4   MAN/DAYS                              │
│                                                           │
│   COMPLETION  DATE: 13TH JUNE 1969                        │
│                                                           │
│   DOCUMENTATION  AMENDED? ✓                               │
│                                                           │
│                                                           │
│   SENIOR  PROGRAMMER: H.W.                                │
│                                                           │
└─────────────────────────────────────────────────────────┘
```

Fig. 14

long it is expected to take. Finally, the third section records the completion of the work.

If the amendment involves rewriting any modules, a normal module description form is made out for each module to be rewritten.

In all cases, both with rewritten and amended modules, normal test data preparation, desk checking and module testing is performed.

Similarly, the senior programmer knits the revised modules together and carries out program testing. With major modifications the senior programmer may also carry out suite testing using revised systems test data.

Finally, the senior programmer must satisfy himself that all documentation is completely up to date. If he judges that further work is needed, either to improve a correction that had to be done hastily, or to rewrite any of the programs in the interests of efficiency, he should bring this to the attention of the programming office manager. This long-term maintenance can then be included in the schedule of development work to be done.

To summarise program maintenance: the suite of programs is designed to carry out a particular job efficiently. As details of the job change and the programs are amended so there is a loss of efficiency. Inevitably, the programs' structures weaken to the point at which it is necessary to write a new suite of programs to do the new job.

What planned and controlled maintenance can achieve is to slow down this degeneration. This prolongs the program's useful life, makes maintenance easier and reduces the number of errors to be corrected.

7. Planning and Control

The basic principle of planning and controlling programming work is to divide the work to be done into a number of small units and to deal with each unit separately.

As a general rule, the unit of work should not be scheduled to take a programmer less than two, or more than five, working days. Furthermore, the smallest unit for planning and measuring should be half a working day. It is futile to attempt to estimate how long a job will take in units smaller than this, and so, although it is possible to record how programmers spend their time hour by hour, there is no point in doing so.

Of course, the units of work should be well chosen; there is no point in giving a programmer three and a half days for a particular job unless it is absolutely clear where the job begins and ends, so that it can be seen whether he has completed it. When modular programming is adopted, such a unit, the module, is readily available.

It is perhaps worth contrasting these principles with much present-day practice. It is still relatively unusual to find any attempt at planning and controlling work in units smaller than the program. A programmer is given, perhaps, ten weeks work to do, and it is only in about the eighth week that there is any clear indication of whether the schedule will be kept or not. By contrast, in modular programming, the same amount of work would be divided into, say, ten pieces with a time estimate for each. Not only does this enable progress to be checked each week; it also introduces some urgency into the situation. Faced with ten weeks work, most people tend to take a week off, or at least to work in a leisurely way, wasting time on irrelevant side issues. However, with a target date only a week away, the job gets done.

There are two other preliminary points to make about the job of controlling and scheduling programming work. Firstly, no programming work of any kind, development or maintenance, must be undertaken until an estimate of the time required has been made and written down. Secondly, time spent

58

must similarly be recorded. Accuracy in estimation increases with practice, and comparing the outcome with the original plan provides valuable feedback and improves future estimates. Programmers sometimes give the impression that their work is too complex and subtle to be subjected to this kind of treatment. Obviously, there is some justice in this. The accuracy obtainable in scheduling programming work is limited by the fact that no two programming tasks are ever exactly the same. On the other hand, accuracy to within ten or fifteen per cent is consistently attainable, provided that estimates are regularly made and regularly checked against what actually happens.

7.2 TIME MEASUREMENTS

It is necessary to distinguish between three different time measurements for each task: standard time, allocated time and actual time.

Standard Time. This is an estimate of how long, to the nearest half day, the task would take the normal programmer. It is not possible to define the normal programmer with any precision, but clearly he should be of adequate ability with adequate training and adequate experience, both in the programming language and in programming methods.

It must be stressed that these standards for the normal programmer are not nearly as precise as those that are frequently developed by work study engineers on the shop floor. One would have to think very carefully before using the programmers' performance against these standards as the basis for any kind of incentive scheme.

Allocated Time. This is the time allocated on the programming office work schedule to a particular task. Normally, it is the same as the standard time, but it may be different, if for example, an inexperienced programmer is expected to fall below the standard. Also, allocated time may include a safety margin, even if experienced programmers do the work.

Actual Time. Obviously, this is the time actually taken by the programmer to do the job in question. Unlike standard and allocated time, it is calculated after the event.

A simple example will make clear the significance of standard, allocated and actual time. Suppose that a set of modules for a particular project are written by two programmers. Adding times for different tasks together, the plan for the next month might look like this:

59

	Tom	Dick	*Total*
Standard Time for work planned	20	20	40
Allocated Time	22	22	44

All figures are in working days; weekends and holidays are excluded. At the end of the month, the picture might be:

	Tom	Dick	*Total*
Standard Time for work planned	20	20	40
Allocated Time	22	22	44
Standard Time for work done	30	15	45
Actual Time	22	15	37

This differs in two ways from the preceding table. Firstly, standard time for work done has been added. This means that the work that Tom actually did this month had a standard time of thirty days, that is, it was expected to occupy a normal programmer for thirty days; the work that Dick did had a standard time of fifteen days. Secondly, actual time has been added, twenty-two and fifteen days respectively.

What emerges from this is that Tom has achieved more, and Dick less, than was planned. However, the reasons are different. Tom was scheduled to do twenty days' work in twenty-two days; in fact he has done thirty days' work in twenty-two days, working at 137 per cent efficiency. Dick, on the other hand, was not able to spend the allocated twenty-two days on the project, but during the fifteen days he did spend on it, he worked at 100 per cent efficiency, producing fifteen days' work.

The point is that, in total, the project received only thirty-seven of the forty-four man days allocated to it, because Dick lost seven days. The reason for this is not stated, but it might be that he was ill or that he had to make an emergency modification to an existing program. This will have to be considered when scheduling for the future; so far the project has not suffered, but only because Tom did more work than was planned.

This leads to the next major point: planning and control needs to be oriented to project and also to the office as a whole.

Project control. For each major development project a weekly report is required showing how work is progressing. It answers questions like: how much of the work has been done? Is it, in fact, receiving the resources allocated to it? Will the target date be met?

Office control. A monthly report is needed on the programming office as a whole. This answers questions like: How are the available resources being used? How much on development? How much on maintenance? How much on training? And how does all this compare with what was planned?

Furthermore, this report should provide information on the individual programmers, how they spend their time and how their performance compares with the standards set.

This then is the basis of the scheduling and control systems. What follows, is, first, an account of the estimation methods, and then an account of the control methods used.

7.3 PLANNING DEVELOPMENT WORK

It may sometimes be necessary to make a crude estimate of the time it will take to implement a suite of programs before the suite has been planned. Where possible, however, the specification should be examined in detail and checked, the job divided into programs and the files designed, before any estimate is made.

What follows is a set of suggested standards; they will almost certainly need adjustment to fit particular circumstances.

First, for each program estimate:

N—The number of source language statements in the program in units of 100 statements. $N = 1$ indicates 100 statements; $N = 3$ indicates 300 statements and so on.

M—The expected number of modules in a program. Of course, this will remain an estimate only until the program has actually been divided into modules.

D—The difficulty of a program on a 3 point scale. $1 = $ easy; $2 = $ normal; $3 = $ difficult.

As a check, N should be multiplied by 100 and divided by M to see if the result, the average number of statements per module, looks reasonable.

Then, an estimate is made of the time needed for the senior programmer's work in each program. The following jobs should be considered separately:

Program planning. That is dividing the program into modules and setting up a list of external variables. Allow first $\frac{1}{2}$, 1 or $1\frac{1}{2}$ days for basic planning, depending on whether the program has $D = 1$, 2, or 3. Then allow time for setting up the external variables; half a day for every hundred statements. Finally, allow one day for every four modules; this is for module documentation. The complete formula is:

Program planning time $= D/2 + N/2 + M/4$
e.g., if $N = 5$, i.e., 500 source language statements

M = 10, i.e., 10 modules

D = 2, i.e., normal difficulty

The time required = 6 days.

Designing program test data. Allow one day.

Program trials. Allow one trial for each point on the D scale and in addition one trial for every ten modules. For each trial, allow a quarter of a day, but in total allow at least one day.

Number of program trials = $D + M/10$

Number of days $\quad = \frac{1}{4}(D + M/10)$ or 1, whichever is greater.

For the program described above, allow therefore three trials and one day.

Operating instructions. Allow one day.

After estimating the senior programmer's work, estimate the junior programmers' work, using M, the estimated number of modules. Allow two days and one trial for each new module:

Total module writing and testing time = $2M$

Total number of trials = M

Allow half a day and one trial for each module that has already been written.

To summarise, the time for the program mentioned previously, where $N = 5, M = 10, D = 2$, is:

	Senior Programmer	Junior Programmers
Program planning	6	–
Program test data	1	–
Module writing and testing	–	20
Program trials	1	–
Operating instructions	1	–
Total	9	20

This example is interesting in various ways. First, it is scheduled to take twenty-nine man/days to produce a 500-statement program at an overall rate of seventeen to eighteen statements per day. This accords well with other estimation methods. Secondly, the figures of nine man/days for the senior and twenty man/days for the junior programmers indicate that one senior programmer can, on average, keep about two juniors fully employed. Finally, it is worth noting that writing the program could take as much as twenty-nine working days, if only one junior programmer works on it; or, assuming

PROGRAMMING TIME ESTIMATE

SUITE: *Sales accounting*

PROGRAM: *Data vet*

SENIOR PROGRAMMER: *Dick*

		STD	REVISED STD	ACTUAL	
NUMBER OF STATEMENTS	N	5		5	
NUMBER OF MODULES	M	10		11	
DIFFICULTY	D	2		/	
PROGRAM PLANNING	D/2+N/2 +M/4	6		5	✓
PROGRAM TEST DATA	I	1		1	✓
MODULE WRITING AND TESTING	2M	20	23	22	✓
PROGRAM TESTING	$\frac{1}{4}$(D+M/10)	1		1	✓
OPERATING INSTRUCTIONS	I	1		1	✓
TOTAL		29	32	28	
NUMBER OF MODULE TESTS	M	10	11	12	
NUMBER OF PROGRAM TESTS	D+M/10	3		2	

START DATE: *June 2nd*

SCHEDULED COMPLETION DATE: *June 25 th.*

ACTUAL COMPLETION: *June 27th.*

Fig. 15

that five junior programmers are made available, as little as thirteen calendar days.

Nothing has been said so far about scheduling the three final tasks that relate to the whole suite: suite trials, operational trials and job appraisal. A great many variables come into play here and it is suggested that estimates are based on the senior programmer's experience.

This, then completes the method for estimating the work content of the job before each program is divided into modules. It is worth checking the estimates for writing and testing the modules when the division has been performed.

Number of statements	0–30	31–70	71–100
Days	1	2	4
Trials	1	1	2

Any necessary adjustments can then be made to the schedule.

The time estimates for a program are summarised on a sheet of paper, see Figure 15. The schedule for a suite of programs is best expressed on a conventional bar chart.

7.4 PLANNING MAINTENANCE WORK

In maintenance work, time estimates are made for the senior programmer's work in designing replacement modules and testing the amended program, and for the junior programmers' work in re-writing and amending the modules concerned. When a module requires re-writing, the estimation methods described in the previous section can be employed. Otherwise informal methods should be used. In fact, it is much less difficult to estimate time required for maintenance work than for development work; there is a solid basis on which to build.

7.5 PROGRAMMERS' TIME RECORDS

Every week, each programmer fills in a document showing how he has spent his time, in units of half a day.

Firstly, non-programming activities are noted, then the balance is shown allocated to the different applications and to the different tasks.

Against each completed task, the standard time for that task is shown. Unfinished tasks have no standard time marked against them. Thus, if in one week a programmer spends two days on a task with a standard time of five days but does not complete it, his form is marked:

2   –

PROGRAMMER'S TIME RECORD

NAME: *TOM*
WEEK ENDING: *JUNE 14ᵀᴴ*

	ACTUAL	STANDARD	COMPLETE
TIME AVAILABLE	5		
HOLIDAY			
SICKNESS	1		
TRAINING			
TOTAL NON-PROGRAMMING TIME	1		
NEW MODULE M09 FOR INVOICING PROGRAM	2	2½	
TOTAL MAINTENANCE TIME	2	2½	
PROGRAM P03-M01	1	2	✓
M03	1		
TOTAL DEVELOPMENT TIME	2	2	

Fig. 16

If in the following week he spends two more days on the task and now completes it (in one day less than the standard time) he marks his form:

2   5

The effect is that, when assessing how far a particular project has advanced, a conservative figure is calculated. If this is felt to be a disadvantage, the alternative is to make the programmers estimate each week what proportion of each unfinished task has been accomplished. In the example given above the programmers' record might read in Week 1:

2   2

and in Week 2:

2   3

In general, however, the former method is recommended.

These times record the basis of the control system. An example of such a form is given in Figure 16.

7.6 WEEKLY PROJECT CONTROL

Figure 17 gives an example of the use of a weekly project progress summary. Originally 120 man/days were allocated to preparing a suite of programs with a total standard time of 111 man/days. The completion date was originally July 4th.

Since then, it has been discovered that the estimate of 111 man/days was too low. Perhaps when dividing a program into modules, the Senior Programmer discovered that it was larger than he had previously estimated. In consequence, this work in standard days has, at some time, been increased to 122 man/days and the time allocation to 130 man/days.

So far, a total of 60 + 20 man/days of the time allocated has been used up, and 58 + 17 standard man/days of work have been achieved. This leaves 50 man/days (= 130 − 60 − 20) in which to achieve forty-seven standard man/days (= 122 − 58 − 17) of work. However, it should be noted that not all of the allocated time is, in the event, being spent on the project. Of the 60 days allocated so far, only fifty-five have actually been spent on the project; five have been lost to other activities.

In future, it is expected that 11 man/days will be spent on the project each week. These, for example, might be two full-time programmers and one half-time programmer on the project. They will do $12\frac{1}{2}$ man/days of work per week between them. Assuming that they lose $\frac{1}{2}$ day per week each to other activities 11 man/days per week are left.

The final calculation shows, therefore, that the project will take 47/11

PROJECT—WEEKLY PROGRESS REPORT

PROJECT: *SALES ACCOUNTING*
WEEK ENDING: *JUNE 7TH 1969*

	TOTALS		PROJECT TO DATE		FUTURE
	ORIGINAL ESTIMATE	PRESENT ESTIMATE	PREVIOUS WEEKS	THIS WEEK	
ALLOCATED DAYS	120	130	60	20	50
ACTUAL DAYS	/////	/////	55	18	/////
WORK IN STD DAYS	111	122	58	17	47
				DAYS AHEAD/BEHIND	3

ORIGINAL COMPLETION DATE: *JULY 4TH*

EXPECTED FUTURE CAPACITY: *11 MAN/DAYS PER WEEK*

EXPECTED TIME TO COMPLETION: *5 WEEKS*

EXPECTED COMPLETION DATE: *JULY 11TH*

Fig. 17

weeks to complete, or between four and five weeks. The figure of five is used to allow for some tailing-off of resources at the end of the project.

7.7 PROGRAMMING OFFICE CONTROL

Figure 18 shows the main programming office control document. Every four weeks the programming office manager plans in detail for the next four weeks. At the top of the form is entered the total capacity; for normal five-day week working, this will be the number of programmers times five. Time lost to other activities is analysed and totalled. The remaining capacity is then allocated to development and maintenance programming, four weekly totals are calculated and also any balance of unallocated time.

As work proceeds, at the end of each week, actual time is entered together with standard days achieved. Thus, at the end of four weeks, a complete summary is available and can be used as a guide for the future.

As an example of the use of this document, first consider Figure 18. This represents the situation at the beginning of a four-week period; the programming office manager has recorded how he intends to use his resources in the next four weeks.

He has six programmers; this makes thirty man/days per week available to him, or 120 man/days over the four weeks. This capacity is entered in the top row of the form and is allocated to different tasks.

First, he notes that one programmer will be on holiday in weeks two and three; he therefore loses five man/days in each week. Similarly, another programmer will be attending a two-week training course in weeks three and four.

A total, then, of twenty man/days out of 120 are expected to be lost in the four weeks. The remaining 100 man/days are allocated to programming work.

There are three programming tasks to be done: The sales accounting suite must be completed; the depot control suite must be begun and the stock recording suite needs amendment. Unfortunately, the specification for the depot control suite will not be ready until week three; although both the other jobs can be finished before the end of week two. In consequence, there are five spare man/days in week two which cannot be immediately allocated to any task.

The total column shows the overall picture. Of the 120 man/days available, it is intended to spend twenty on non-programming activities, eighty-five on development, ten on maintenance and five are unallocated.

What actually happens? Figure 19 shows how the form might look when it is completed four weeks later. Firstly, examine the 'actual' times.

Holidays and training took place as planned. However, an additional five

PROGRAMMING OFFICE 4-WEEKLY SUMMARY

	W/E 7/6/69			W/E 14/6/69			W/E 21/6/69			W/E 28/6/69			4 WEEK TOTAL		
	ALL	ACT	STD ACH	ALL	ACT	STD ACH	ALL	ACT	STD ACH	ALL	ACT	STD ACH	ALL	ACT	STD ACH
MAN/DAYS AVAILABLE	30			30			30			30			120		
HOLIDAY				5			5						10		
TRAINING							5			5			10		
TOTAL NON-PROGRAMMING	0			5			10			5			20		
SALES ACCOUNTING	25			15									40		
DEPOT CONTROL							20			25			45		
TOTAL DEVELOPMENT	25			15			20			25			85		
STOCK RECORDING	5			5									10		
TOTAL MAINTENANCE	5			5									10		
BALANCE	0	0		5	0		0	0		0	0		5	0	

Fig. 18

69

PROGRAMMING OFFICE 4-WEEKLY SUMMARY														
	W/E 7/6/69			W/E 14/6/69			W/E 21/6/69			W/E 28/6/69			4 WEEK TOTAL		
	ALL	ACT	STD ACH	ALL	ACT	STD ACH	ALL	ACT	STD ACH	ALL	ACT	STD ACH	ALL	ACT	STD ACH
MAN/DAYS AVAILABLE	30	30		30	30		30	30		30	30		120	120	
HOLIDAY				5	5		5	5					10	10	
TRAINING							5	5		5	5		10	10	
SICKNESS										0	5		0	5	
TOTAL NON-PROGRAMMING	0	0		5	5		10	10		5	10		20	25	
SALES ACCOUNTING	25	22	20	15	20	13							40	42	33
DEPOT CONTROL							20	17	19	25	17	23	45	34	42
TOTAL DEVELOPMENT	25	22	20	15	20	13	20	17	19	25	17	23	85	76	75
STOCK RECORDING	5	5	5	5	5	5							10	10	10
PAYROLL	0	3	4				0	3	3	0	3	3	0	9	10
TOTAL MAINTENANCE	5	8	9	5	5	5	0	3	3	0	3	3	10	19	20
BALANCE	0	0		5	0		0	0		0	0		5	0	

Fig. 19

70

man/days were lost to sickness in week four. Besides this, the payroll suite gave trouble and a total of nine man/days were needed during the four weeks to put it right. Note that, in his original plan, the programming office manager did not allocate any time to this kind of 'fire-fighting' maintenance; it would have been better had he done so. The amendment to the stock recording suite went as planned; the sales accounting suite was completed almost as planned; but the new depot control suite received only thirty-four of the allocated forty-five man/days.

In addition the programming work achieved, measured in standard days, is recorded. This reveals that the forty-two man/days spent completing the sales accounting suite only accomplished thirty-three standard man/days work. By contrast, the depot control suite has forged ahead; the thirty-four man/days spent on it were very effective, as forty-two standard days' work were done. In fact, this report needs to be supplemented by a report showing the performance of each programmer measured against standard times.

A final point to note is that this report and the weekly project report complement each other. The four-weekly summary does not attempt to indicate whether or not targets will be met, but it does, on the other hand, give a good picture of how resources were utilised and how efficiently.

7.8 PLANNING AND CONTROL—SUMMARY

This chapter has concentrated on describing the basic documents needed for planning and control. Almost certainly, bar charts of one kind or another will be useful as a way of displaying visually what is happening. As a minimum, the computer steering committee, if there is one, should be given the programming office control document, together with the latest progress reports on current development projects.

There are various percentages that can very usefully be calculated. For the office as a whole, what percentage is standard time of actual time? Of the total capacity, what percentages are spent on non-programming activities, maintenance and development respectively? The maintenance percentage, when calculated, nearly always surprises management by being higher than expected.

Finally, it must be added that anybody reading this, who comes from outside the computer field, will be surprised at the very primitive planning and control methods here recommended. The fact is that this is a very neglected subject; planning of some kind is now almost universal, but effective control is rare. How often do you see a six-month-old bar chart pinned to the programming office wall, which has never been touched since the first flush of optimism?

71

Success in controlling programming is largely a matter of attitude; once a serious attempt to do so is made, it is found that relatively blunt instruments will produce excellent results. However, there is no doubt that the methods described here can be refined, and it seems likely that learning curve methodology will soon be applied to programming.